Recipes from OHIO's Must Places to Eat

Recipes from OHIO's Must Places to Eat

A COLLECTION OF FAMOUS FAVORITES
FROM THE **RESTAURANT TRAVEL GUIDE**
Eating Your Way Across Ohio

Karen A. Patterson

AP™
Acclaim Press
MORLEY, MISSOURI

Acclaim Press
— Your Next Great Book —
P.O. Box 238
Morley, MO 63767
(573) 472-9800
www.acclaimpress.com

Book Design by:
Steward & Wise
GRAPHIC DESIGN

Cover Design by M. Frene Melton

Copyright © 2015, Karen A. Patterson
All Rights Reserved.

No part of this book shall be reproduced or transmitted in any form or by any means, electronic or mechanical, including photocopying, recording or by an information or retrieval system, except in the case of brief quotations embodied in articles and reviews, without the prior written consent of the publisher. The scanning, uploading, and distribution of this book via the Internet or via any other means without permission of the publisher is illegal and punishable by law.

ISBN-10: 1-938905-62-8
ISBN-13: 978-1-938905-62-9
Library of Congress Control Number: 2014907473

First Printing: 2015
Printed in the United States of America
10 9 8 7 6 5 4 3 2 1

This publication was produced using available information.
The publisher regrets it cannot assume responsibility for errors or ommisions.

Contents

Introduction

"My vision is not only to define food and cooking as an art, but to go back to the roots of cooking and showcase the process through a more simplistic, ethereal approach as an expression of life and living." **(Lorena Garcia, a leading Latina chef)**

Food is without a doubt an essential part of life. It sustains us physically, but it also helps us commemorate significant social events. Down through history and in most every culture food has been at the center of gatherings where people celebrate, pay tribute, observe religious rites and participate in traditional ceremonies.

Not only does nourishment comfort our souls, it represents the ethnic heritage of cultures around the globe. In Ohio, we are the beneficiaries of this rich heritage because of the diversity of restaurants that are available for our eating pleasure.

While researching my first book, *Eating Your Way Across Ohio: 101 Must Places to Eat,* in this Ohio travel series, I visited over 160 locally owned and managed restaurants in order to choose 101 of the best in the state. I enjoyed sampling a wide variety of ethnic cuisine including Mediterranean, Mexican, Oriental, Greek, and French in establishments as diverse as cafes and diners, as well as bistros and five-star restaurants. It was an exciting experience which resulted in taste-tested recommendations for Ohio's hungry travelers.

Since the book's release, many of my readers have reported that the search for these eateries has been half the fun, like a scavenger hunt, as they travelled throughout the state. Once they arrived, they found the food, atmosphere and service most rewarding and worth the search. Often they have the staff sign the book and mark each entry with their receipt. The owners and managers have also reported that the book has given a much appreciated boost to their business. So it has been a win-win outcome all the way around.

In this second book, *Recipes from Ohio's Must Places to Eat: A Collection of Famous Favorites from the Restaurant Travel Guide,* I wanted to share with my readers some of the tantalizing dishes featured at these restaurants. So I have gathered over 200 recipes from those tried and true places featured in the *Eating Your Way Across Ohio* book, and included many tasty favorites from family and friends.

Of course, there is nothing that replaces the comfortable ambiance, the attentive service and the exquisite flavor of the actual dish in the restaurant where it was created, so grab a copy of *Eating Your Way Across Ohio*, spend a day or two checking out the featured restaurants and enjoy the beautiful Ohio countryside. Until you are able to get on the road, however, try these recipes at home.

Please note that the recipes presented in this book were supplied by the featured restaurants and any similarity to copyrighted recipes is simply coincidental since many dishes have the same ingredients and often similar measurements.

I hope this book helps you expand your culinary skills and your gastronomic experience. Bon Appetit!

Acknowledgments

When I am asked what I do when I am not teaching, I reply that I write. All too often people tell me that they should or are going to write a book about their lives. No doubt there are many lives out there that are worth writing and reading about, but writing can be demanding and tedious. The 20th century poet and author, Dorothy Parker said, "I hate writing, but I love having written." And at times I agree with her. The process requires discipline and patience to work for hours searching for the most precise words and to assemble them into comprehensive sentences, like a jigsaw puzzle, to convey the desired message.

The process, however, is much easier with the support of family and friends who pitch in when I'm under a deadline or cheer me on when the task at hand seems impossible. I am fortunate to have so many dedicated "supporters" and I appreciate their thoughtfulness.

My main cheerleader is my husband John who checks on my progress frequently and offers help whenever I need an extra hand or set of eyes to proofread copy. We have made a good life together for more than a quarter of a century and share four children, four grandchildren and a few great-grandbabies. As my best friend, he has had his steady hand on the helm and has guided us through some mighty rough waters over the years.

Vicki Nichols is the newest addition to my group of supporters and has added balance to my deadline-oriented life. She keeps me on schedule and, as a detail person, she remembers most everything that I have forgotten. Vicki has been an immense help in getting this book to the finish line for which I am most grateful.

Karen Raybould was my trusted travelling pal during my research trips for the *Eating Your Way Across Ohio* book, and she graciously offered to help, once again, in following up with restaurants to collect their recipes. Her outgoing personality exudes warmth which has been a real plus when we met with so many managers and owners.

Living on a small homestead with a routine of daily chores and a variety of animals to care for can often be overwhelming especially when there is not enough time in the day to get it all done. My dear friend, Jan Head, generously gave her time to help me with my annual task of putting in the garden. She spent countless hours helping me plant, cultivate, and weed not one but both gardens, thus freeing up more of my time so that I could finish this book. She is always someone that I can depend on. Thank you, Jan!

Another new member of the team is Sandy Yoakam. As a professional proofreader for many years, she came out of retirement to work with me and for that I am so grateful. She has an eye for picking out errors in the text and did a great job of catching mine.

I don't know what I would do without my resident technical support man, my son, Jesse Paschke, who often had to retrieve documents sitting on a cloud somewhere in cyberspace. Since computers have a mind of their own and get hung up, form glitches or even crash when I least expect it, usually when I'm under a deadline, Jesse came to my rescue frequently.

I must also thank the many restaurant managers and owners who so generously provided me with some of their prized recipes. Without their cooperation, this book would not be possible.

And, finally, it has been a pleasure to work with Keith Steele, Randy Baumgardner and the staff at Acclaim Press. They have demonstrated professionalism on every level and their knowledge and expertise in the publishing business has resulted in the production of many exquisite books.

Dedication

To John, My Beloved Forever

Recipes from OHIO's Must Places to Eat

A COLLECTION OF FAMOUS FAVORITES
FROM THE **RESTAURANT TRAVEL GUIDE**
Eating Your Way Across Ohio

NORTH WEST REGION

Azula Tequila Napoleon, OH

Briarfield Café Maumee, OH

Cabbage Patch Restaurant Defiance, OH

Dock's Beach House Port Clinton, OH

Greek Garden Findlay, OH

Happy Daz Lima, OH

Kermit's Bowling Green, OH

Le Petit Gourmet Maumee, OH

The Orchard Tree Van Wert, OH

Welcome Home Family Dining Bryan, OH

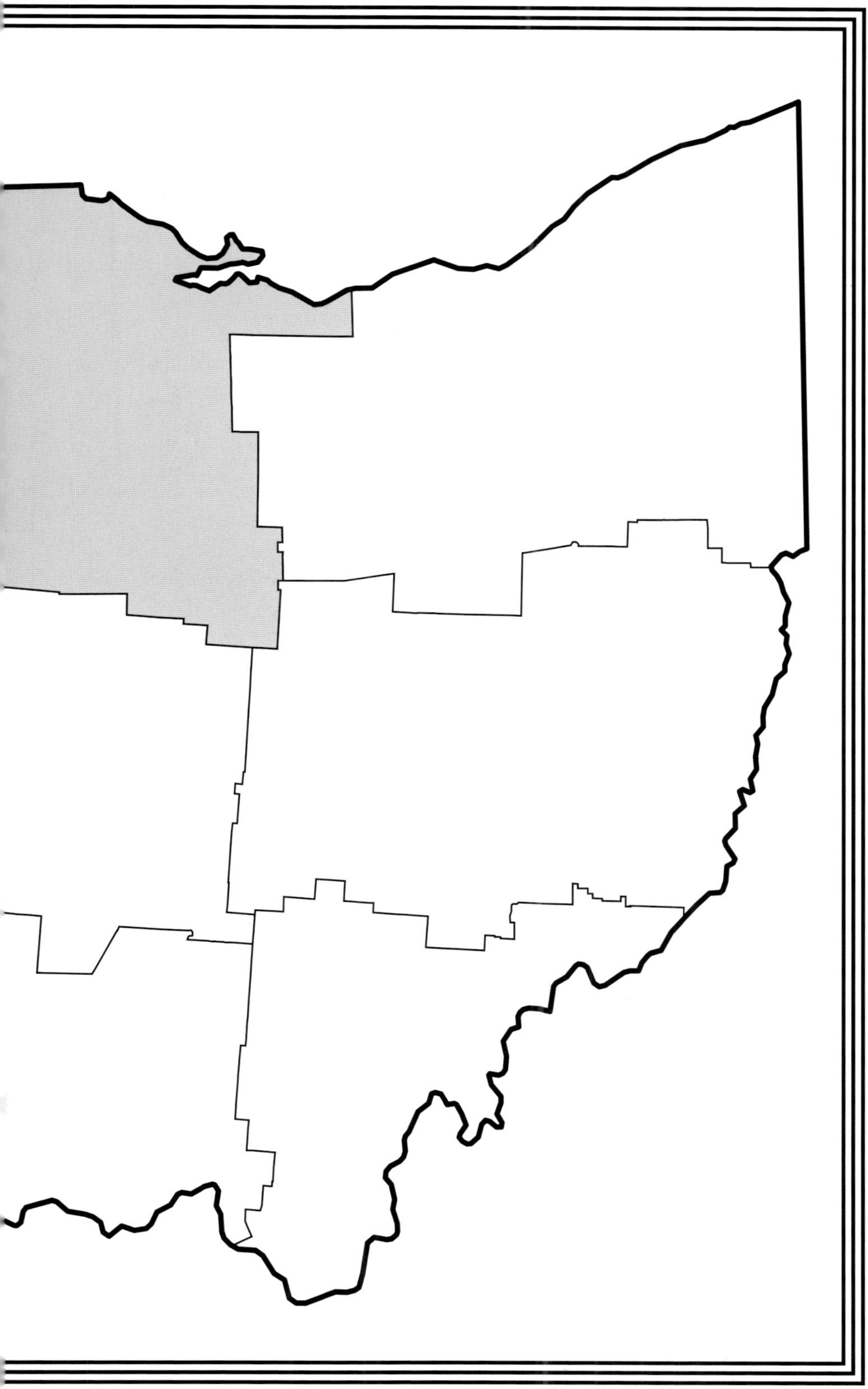

Azula Tequila

Napoleon, OH

601 E. Riverview Avenue
Napoleon, OH 43545
419-599-9028
www.azul-tequila.com

Emmanuel Ramirez is a shining star to his family and friends back in his hometown of Arandas, about an hour from Guadalajara, Mexico. He has worked hard since arriving in the U.S. as a teenager and finally fulfilled his dream of creating a restaurant where he can showcase his family's recipes. Azula is one of the few Mexican restaurants in the area and Emmanuel has created an elegant yet casual atmosphere.

When I asked him to share some of his recipes, he hesitated. After all, he had come a long way with his family's blessings and a treasure trove of authentic Mexican recipes. But he did share two that are an important part of many of his dishes. So here they are. This gives you a start. Use your own creative genius and add creamy guacamole or mild to spicy salsa to enhance your Mexican menu.

Fresh Guacamole

2 avocados, ripe and soft
½ onion, chopped
⅛ teaspoon jalapeno peppers
1 medium tomato, chopped
Lime juice
Salt

Mash the flesh of the avocados so that all lumps are removed and the pulp is a smooth texture. Add the chopped onions and peppers. Gently fold the tomatoes into the mixture being careful not to crush them. Add a few drops of lime to offset the sweet flavor of the avocado. Salt to taste. Serve with most any Mexican dish.

Salsa Mexicana (Pico de Gallo)

1 cup onions, chopped
2½ cups tomatoes, chopped
Cilantro, finely chopped
Jalapeno or serrano peppers, minced
lime juice

Combine chopped onions and tomatoes and mix together. Add fresh cilantro. Spice up the flavor with either jalapeno or the meatier and hotter serrano pepper, depending on your taste. Add a few drops of lime juice and salt to taste.

Briarfield Cafe

Maumee, OH

3220 Briarfield Boulevard
Maumee, OH 43537
(419) 865-7260
www.briarfieldcafe.com

This convenient café, located on Briarfield Avenue in Maumee, is a great place for lunch and dinner. But the breakfast menu, which is offered all day beginning at 7:00 a.m., is particularly appealing with its wide variety of choices. A few of the breakfast specialties are variations of French Toast (Pecan Caramel, Cinnamon Swirl, and Banana), and a delicious and filling Breakfast Pizza. Any breakfast lover would surely find a favorite on this menu.

Owners Jude and Dave Katafiasz are a charming couple and warmly welcomed me when I visited. They also provided me with the breakfast of a lifetime, allowing me to sample many of their specials. It was hard to choose what I liked the most, but since their twist on French Toast is so unique and delicious, I thought I would share a French Toast recipe that should knock the sleepy seeds from the eyes of your house guests.

French Toast

9 eggs
2 cups cream
1½ teaspoons nutmeg
1½ teaspoons cinnamon
½ cup butter, melted and cooled
8 to 10 slices of bread
Powdered sugar
Fresh bananas, sliced (optional)
Maple syrup, warm (optional)

Crack the eggs into a large bowl and beat with a wire whisk. Add cream, nutmeg and cinnamon, and blend the flavors. While whisking, pour in the melted butter and stir every so often to combine with the egg mixture. Heat the griddle or skillet until a few drops of water sizzle and quickly evaporate when sprinkled on the surface.

Use day-old bread, if available, because it is firmer and holds up better in the mixture. Dunk the bread into the egg mixture and let it soak for only a few seconds until evenly coated. If left too long it will become soggy which will make the bread difficult to handle, breaking apart before it is grilled. Drain off excess mixture and place on the hot griddle.

Cook until golden brown on the first side, about 3 to 4 minutes, then flip over to the other side. Continue to cook the other side for about 2 minutes. Remove and place sliced fresh bananas either on top or as garnish, and sprinkle with powdered sugar. Serve with warm maple syrup.

Cabbage Patch Carry Out

Defiance, OH

19492 State Route 637
Defiance, OH 43512
(419) 393-2271

At one time there was only a restaurant at this location, but Cabbage Patch is now a carry-out and gas station that was built right beside the restaurant which is under new ownership.

Conveniently located on State Route 637 near the Auglaize River, drop by this new one-stop spot to gas up and to pick up snacks, pizza, Breakfast Tornados, hot dogs, or a grab-and-go lunch special. There are also fine meats available including T-bone and Delmonico steaks, ground beef, and sausage as well as a variety of cheeses (Colby, Colby Jack and Hot Pepper).

If you like to live on the wild side, Buffalo Bob's Big Game jerky and meat sticks are sold in bulk as well as singles. And some of their exotic meats include alligator, venison, buffalo, ostrich, kangaroo, wild boar and elk. On the tamer side, owner Kathy Schlegel shared a few of her favorite sweet recipes.

Apple Crumb Pie

2/3 cup sugar
2 teaspoons flour
¾ teaspoon cinnamon
6 to 8 medium apples, sliced
9 inch pie shell – home made or commercially prepared
Ice cream

Topping
½ cup flour
¼ cup sugar
¼ cup butter, softened

Preheat oven to 400 degrees. Combine the sugar, flour and cinnamon in a bowl and then stir in the apples being carefully not to break the slices. Spread into a prepared pie shell and gently press down on the mixture in order to compact it before adding the topping. Mix the flour, sugar and butter together so that it has the texture of small crumbles and sprinkle evenly over the apples. Bake for 45 to 50 minutes. Serve warm and top with a scoop of ice cream if desired .

Nutty Haystacks

½ cup sugar
½ cup of light Karo syrup
½ cup peanut butter
2 cups chow mein noodles, Rice Chex, Corn Chex or corn flakes cereal
Wax paper

Mix sugar, Karo and peanut butter in a pan and heat slowly on medium heat until it gently boils.

Stir constantly. Fold in the noodles or cereal and mix thoroughly. Remove from stove and drop spoon size dollops onto wax paper about an inch apart. Cool to allow them to set and then serve.

Dock's Beach House Bar & Grille

Port Clinton, OH

252 West Lakeshore Drive
Port Clinton, OH 43452
(419) 732-6609
www.docksbeachhouse.com

Dock's is one of my favorite places to visit in Port Clinton. Not only does it feature one of the most picturesque locations along Lake Erie, but its casual atmosphere provides a perfect setting for a lazy afternoon on the expansive deck or the adjoining beach where you can leisurely eat and drink as the waves tickle your toes.

Each time I have visited, I have had a great meal and a relaxing time just watching the waves roll in. In fact, my husband and I usually stay at the Commodore Perry Inn conveniently located across the street from Dock's. The rooms are clean and spacious, and the upper floors have a scenic view of the lake.

In the summer, Port Clinton is alive with activity and is only a short ferry ride to the islands where Lake Erie takes on a different persona from the mainland. But Dock's closes from October to May for the winter.

Dock's creamy Lobster Bisque is quite tasty with large chunks of lobster. Their thick steaks are tender and juicy, too. On the lighter side, I enjoy their wraps which are usually served with a generous helping of couscous.

The following recipes are good examples of what you can expect when you visit.

Peppercorn New York Strip Steak

4 10-ounce New York strip steaks
1 tablespoon kosher salt
1 tablespoon cracked black pepper
1 tablespoon granulated garlic

Combine salt, pepper and garlic until thoroughly blended then rub the mixture on both sides of the steak so that the seasoning infuses the meat. Grill at 400 degrees for 5 to 6 minutes on each side for medium rare. Adjust the time for rare or well done options. Serve with Aged Balsamic Reduction and Bleu Cheese crumbles (see below).

Aged Balsamic Reduction:
1 cup aged Balsamic vinegar
Bleu cheese crumbles

In order to reduce the vinegar by half its liquid content, pour it into a shallow pan and place on medium heat. Stir constantly until the excess liquid in the vinegar evaporates to half the original amount. This remaining liquid is thicker and has a more concentrated flavor that complements the meat. Drizzle desired amount over each steak before serving and top with Bleu cheese crumbles.

Citrus and Ancho Pepper Marinated T-Bone Pork Chops

10 T-bone pork chops, ¾ inch thick or 14 to 16 ounces each
2 small cans ancho chilies in adobo sauce
Juice of 2 oranges
1 cup brown sugar
2 cups olive oil
1 tablespoon oregano, dried
1 tablespoon thyme, dried

Puree all ingredients together in a blender except for the meat. Pour the mixture over the pork chops in a bowl and refrigerate for one hour. Turn the chops and let sit in the mixture for an additional hour in the refrigerator. Grill 8 to 10 minutes on each side and finish in the oven on 450 degrees for 5 to 6 minutes. Top with a favorite barbecue sauce.

Greek Garden

Findlay, OH

321 South Main Street
Findlay, OH 45840
(419) 422-0808
www.thegreekgarden.com

Findlay boasts of a thriving downtown where distinctive shops catch the eye and attention of visitors and exceptional restaurants satisfy a host of eating preferences. This level of activity seems to be creating a buzz of excitement in the area not often found today in small town America where the heart of most communities used to be centered.

One excellent restaurant is the Greek Garden, which is a colorful themed place located in the heart of this prosperous community. But for owner Beau Thompson the theme goes further than décor. He offers authentic Greek cuisine which is a tribute to his heritage. The following recipes are just a delicious sampling from his menu.

Egg Lemon Soup
(Avgolemono Soupa)

1 small whole chicken
10 cups water
1 teaspoon chicken base
¾ cup rice, uncooked
Salt and pepper
1 egg, separated
¼ cup lemon juice
1½ tablespoons corn starch

In a large pot, cover chicken with at least 10 cups of water. Boil until chicken is tender, remove from the pot and when cool, debone and cut into bite sized chunks. Strain 10 cups of broth, reserving one cup to cool. Bring the remaining 9 cups to a boil in a separate pan and add rice, chicken base, salt and pepper. Separate the egg in a bowl. Set aside the yoke then beat the egg white with a mixer at a high speed until it is foamy. Slowly stir in the yolk, lemon juice, 1 cup of cooled broth, and cornstarch and mix thoroughly. Continue to cook the rice until it is tender then fold in the egg-lemon mixture. Boil until the soup thickens, about 3 to 5 minutes, then add chicken chunks. Mix well. Serves 6 to 8.

Tabboulch
(Parsley Wheat Salad)

1 cup cracked bulgur wheat, medium or fine grain
2 large bunches of parsley, chopped
1 cup fresh mint or 1 tablespoon dried mint
1 small bunch of green onions or 1 medium sweet onion, chopped
Juice of 3 lemons
¼ cup oil
Salt and pepper
5 tomatoes, seeded and chopped
1 cucumber, peeled and chopped

Cover bulgur wheat in a bowl of water and soak for 10 minutes. Drain. Combine parsley, mint and chopped onion in a separate bowl and add to the thoroughly drained wheat. Stir lemon juice, oil, salt and pepper together and add to the wheat. Mix well. Cover tightly and refrigerate overnight. Before serving, fold in tomatoes and cucumber. Serves 6.

Beef And Macaroni Casserole
(Pastitsio)

2 pounds penne rigate pasta, cooked
3½ sticks of butter, melted
4 eggs, separated and reserve yolks
½ cup olive oil
½ red onion, diced
2 to 2½ pounds ground lamb or beef
8 ounces tomato sauce
1 cup water
1 tablespoon salt
1 teaspoon pepper

<u>Bechamel Sauce</u>
6 cups whole milk
1 cup flour

1 to 2 cups bread crumbs
2 cups Parmesan cheese, grated

Preheat oven to 350 degrees. Toss cooked pasta with half the butter. Whisk the egg whites until stiff and fold into the pasta. Set aside. Reserve the yolks. In a large deep frying pan, heat oil and partially caramelize the onions until they are a golden brown. Stir in ground meat and brown, but not completely cooked, about 7 to 10 minutes over medium heat. Break up the meat so there are no large lumps. Stir in tomato sauce, water, salt and pepper and mix thoroughly. Cook for an additional 7 to 10 minutes. Reduce heat and simmer until ready to assemble.

For the Bechamel Sauce, begin by bringing milk to a boil in a medium pan. In a mixing bowl, combine flour with half the remaining butter. Slowly add the hot milk into the butter mixture. Continue to whisk while adding the egg yolks. Pour back into pan, and heat on medium. Whisk for about 5 minutes until consistency is very thick. Remove from the heat and set aside.

Coat the bottom of a large deep baking pan with butter. Layer ½ the bread crumbs, ½ the pasta, 1 cup cheese, ground meat, pasta, Bechamel sauce, cheese and finish with a layer of bread crumbs. Bake 45 minutes.

EAT GREEK & BE MERRY!!!

Happy Daz

Lima, OH

1064 Bellefontaine Avenue
Lima, OH 45804
(419) 227-3663
www.happydaz.com

This is a 1950s diner in the vein of the old television sitcom "Happy Days". The décor features metal stools with red plastic seat covers, round high top tables and a jukebox playing Oldies in the background. Scrumptious desserts are featured in a glass display case and the staff is dressed in the '50s style. The food is nothing fancy, but it is tasty and reasonably priced. The menu also features '50s favorites like the All-Beef Foot Long Coney, the BLT, Breaded or Grilled Pork Tenderloin and Texas Grilled Cheese sandwiches.

As a mashed potato aficionado, I loved the selection of Loaded Mashed Potato Bowls that are chocked full of spiced garlic chicken, baked steak and gravy or chicken with sweet corn and gravy. They are not only filling but totally satisfying; a meal in themselves. I was also impressed with the rich and creamy Mac n' Cheese which is one of their most popular items on the menu. I can understand why because it was one of the best mac n' cheese dishes I've ever tasted. And you can get the same dishes at any of their four locations.

Though their Mac n' Cheese recipe is not public knowledge and will remain a well-kept secret, I have included a variation of the dish that is an old time favorite of mine.

Three Cheese Mac n' Cheese

2 cups of elbow macaroni
Water
½ cup butter
8 ounces each of Cheddar, American and Colby, shredded
1¼ cups light cream
Salt

Preheat the oven to 325 degrees. Place macaroni in a large saucepan, cover with water and cook until barely soft. Drain into a colander, rinse with hot water and set aside. Melt the butter in a pan and blend in the shredded cheeses. Stir until melted. Gradually add the cream continuously stirring until the mixture is thickened. The consistency is important when combined with the macaroni. If it is too thick it will clump up and if it is too thin, it will be soupy. Fold the macaroni into the mixture in the pan until thoroughly coated. Salt to taste and spread into a baking pan. Top with additional cheese. Bake for 30 minutes until thoroughly heated.

Kermit's Family Restaurant

Bowling Green, OH

307 South Main Street
Bowling Green, OH 43402
(419) 354-1388
www.kermitsbg.com

In the heart of downtown Bowling Green, only blocks from the University, there are many dining choices, but I found Kermit's to be a warm, comfortable place to regroup during my travels. I tucked myself into a booth, looked over the menu and found many dishes that were appealing. However, their bestseller, the Tandoories, caught my eye since I was not familiar with this type of dish. From all of the choices of Tandoories, I selected the Greek Chicken. As it turns out, it was excellent with an exotic taste. This flatbread is also the basis for other sandwiches as well. Manager Cassie Mass, the owner's daughter, was very hospitable and provided me with a number of delicious recipes that she thought our readers would enjoy. Thanks Cassie!

Kermit's Applesauce

15 pounds apples
1 tablespoon cinnamon
2 cups white sugar (level)
1 cup brown sugar (level)
4 tablespoons lemon juice
2 cups water

Peel, core and slice apples. Place ½ of the apple slices in medium pan. Sprinkle the cinnamon and 1 cup of white sugar over them. Top with the remaining apples and layer with the rest of the ingredients in the following order: brown sugar, remaining white sugar, lemon juice, and water. Cover with foil and put on the stove over medium to high heat. When it begins to boil, remove foil, turn heat to low, and stir apples. Continue cooking over low heat until apples are soft. Avoid sticking or burning by stirring . Serve warm or cold.

Kermit's Coney Sauce

5 medium onions
2 cloves of garlic
1¼ cups melted margarine
2 bottles of A-1 sauce
½ cup sugar
½ teaspoon salt
1 teaspoon pepper
½ cup mustard
3½ cups salsa
3 tablespoons taco seasoning
5 pounds ground meat
1 24-ounce bottle of ketchup

Puree onions and garlic in food processor. Pour into pan with margarine and cook until translucent. Add A-1 sauce, sugar, salt, pepper, mustard, salsa, and taco seasoning. Stir and cook until thoroughly heated. Brown ground meat in a pan. While it is cooking, chop the meat up to a fine consistency and then drain off the grease. Add meat to the onion mixture along with the ketchup. After emptying the ketchup into the sauce, fill bottle ⅔ full with water, shake and add to the sauce. Stir and heat thoroughly.

Buckeye Pie

This pie filling is a two-step process. The peanut butter layer is made first followed by the chocolate layer, but first prepare the peanut butter mixture that will be added in the first step.

Peanut Butter Mixture
5½ cups powdered sugar
1 16-ounce jar of smooth peanut butter

With a fork, mix powdered sugar and peanut butter together until well blended. It should roughly have the consistency of damp cornmeal.

First Step – Peanut Butter Pie Filling Layer
3 egg yolks
⅙ cup sugar
⅙ cup cornstarch
1 teaspoon vanilla
1½ cups 2% white milk
⅙ cup margarine
1 baked pastry pie shell

In a small sauce pan combine egg yolks, sugar, cornstarch, vanilla, and whisk until smooth. Then slowly add the white milk. Add margarine and place mixture in saucepan over high heat on the stove. Whisk swiftly and continuously until margarine melts, then add heaping ½ cup of the peanut butter mixture. Continue to whisk until mixture thickens to the consistency of pudding. Pour into pie shell.

Second Step – Chocolate Pie Filling Layer

3 egg yolks
1/6 cup sugar
1/6 cup cornstarch
1/6 cup cocoa
1 teaspoon vanilla
1½ cups chocolate milk
1/6 cup margarine
Whipped cream

In small saucepan combine egg yolks, sugar, cornstarch, cocoa, vanilla, and whisk until smooth. Add chocolate milk, and slowly whisk into mixture. Add margarine and place over high heat on stove. Whisk swiftly and continuously until margarine melts, then continue to whisk until mixture thickens to pudding consistency. Spread the chocolate pie filling layer over the peanut butter layer in the pie shell. Sprinkle remaining peanut butter mixture over chocolate layer, and chill. Top with whipped cream and serve.

1000 Island Dressing

½ gallon of Miracle Whip mayonnaise
2 cups sugar
1½ cups ketchup
1 cup sweet pickle relish
2½ cups milk
½ cup onions, finely diced

Blend all the ingredients in the above order in a mixing bowl until it reaches a consistent pinkish color all the way through. Pour in a glass container and store in the refrigerator. Use on salads and burgers. Makes 1 gallon.

Kermit's
family
restaurant
NOW OPEN
UNTIL
8PM
BIGGER
MENU
LONGER
HOURS
SALISBURY STEAK
NOW ACCEPTING
CREDIT CARDS
ICE

Kermit's
family
restaurant
KERMIT S
SHIRTS
AVAILABLE

Le Petit Gourmet

Maumee, OH

6546 Weatherfield Court
Maumee, OH 43537
(419) 866-6343

This is a charming little oasis tucked away in a Maumee industrial park. The building, with its bold and expansive blue and white awnings, distinctive white farm lights dotting the exterior and neat red brick framework, distinguish it from the professional buildings in the area.Even though it stands out, it is still hard to find.

Not only does Le Petit Gourmet provide catering and carry-out meals to area businesses, but walk-in guests can choose from a variety of deli favorites and enjoy their meal at the attractive tables. And the large fireplace creates a cozy atmosphere during the cold winter months.

Quick foods are available, like salads and fajitas, but there are also more substantial sandwiches, such as the Cambell Rae's Filet.

Cambell Rae's Filet

Manager John Kozak provided me with this "best selling sandwich" recipe and added that it is "best eaten alone, silent, and paired with a high quality ale." Sounds more like a mystical experience than a meal!

Vegetable oil
Whole beef tenderloin, silverback removed
3 fresh garlic cloves, minced
1 teaspoon kosher salt
1 tablespoon crushed black pepper
½ white onion, sliced
French baguette
Lettuce, Romaine
Heirloom tomatoes, sliced
Horseradish

Drizzle a little vegetable oil over a whole beef tenderloin. Combine the garlic, salt, and pepper with remaining oil until the mixture has a gritty consistency. Mix thoroughly and rub the mixture over and under the entire piece of meat. Place it in a roasting pan and tuck the onion underneath the meat. Let sit for 45 minutes in order to bring it to room temperature.

In the meantime, preheat oven to 475 degrees and when it has reached temperature place the meat in the oven for 12 minutes. Do not open the oven door once the meat has been placed in the oven. Reduce the oven temperature to 275 degrees. Cook for another 10 to 12 minutes. When finished, take the tenderloin out of the oven and let rest until the internal temperature reaches 120 to 125 degrees.

Place in the fridge for a few hours until it is chilled. Carve in thin slices and serve on a crusty French baguette with fresh Romaine lettuce, heirloom tomatoes, roasted onions from the pan and freshly opened horseradish. John highly recommends pairing this sandwich with a high quality brown ale or porter beer.

Q Sauce

1 cup of ketchup
1 can of Coca Cola
¼ cup cider vinegar
1 teaspoon instant coffee
2 tablespoons molasses
½ teaspoon of hickory liquid smoke
Pinch of salt and pepper

This is an easy recipe and can be used for most anything that needs added flavor or a bit of spice. Mix all ingredients together in a saucepan and cook over a low heat for 30 minutes. Keep stirring to avoid sticking to the pan. When it is a thickened, remove from the heat and place in a glass container. Sauce can keep up to 2 weeks in the refrigerator. Makes about 2 to 3 cups.

The Orchard Tree

Van Wert, OH

1058 West Main Street
Van Wert, OH 45891
(419) 238-5235

I was not familiar with Van Wert and arrived in town tired and hungry, not sure of what I was in the mood to eat. The buffet at the Orchard Tree, however, provided me with so many choices that it was difficult to decide: soup, salad, sandwiches, burgers, and beef or chicken and noodles. I found the selection of items to be fresh because the servers regularly replenished the buffet, especially the popular items, like chicken or fish. As a result I did not find that the food sat too long or was dried out. When I was finished eating, I was able to collect a few of the recipes for items either found on the buffet or on the general menu.

The Papa T's

2 pounds ground beef
1 pound ground pork sausage
3 eggs
½ cup green pepper, diced
½ cup yellow onion, diced
½ cup Mozzarella cheese, shredded
Pepper Jack cheese, sliced
Bacon slices, cooked
Sour dough bread

Mix the beef, sausage, eggs, pepper, onion and Mozzarella cheese together and form 6 ounce patties. Grill or pan fry and top with slices of Pepper Jack cheese and bacon. Serve on sour dough bread.

Taco Soup

5 pounds ground beef
3 4-ounce packages of taco seasoning
1 50-ounce can of tomato soup
1 48-ounce can tomato juice
6 16-ounce cans of kidney beans, drained

4 cans diced tomatoes
Sour cream
Cheddar cheese, shredded
Tortilla chips

Brown ground beef in a pan. Add taco seasoning, tomato soup and tomato juice, kidney beans and diced tomatoes. Simmer mixture on low heat for 30 minutes. Stir frequently until smooth and all ingredients are blended. Top with a dollop of sour cream and sprinkle with Cheddar cheese and serve with a side of tortilla chips.

Sloppy Joes

4 pounds ground beef
1 cup onion, diced
½ cup green pepper, diced
4 cups ketchup
½ cup white sugar
½ cup white vinegar
½ cup yellow mustard
1 teaspoon celery seed
1½ teaspoons Worcestershire sauce
Salt and pepper to taste

Brown ground beef in a pan. Add onion and green pepper. Cook until the onion is transparent and the pepper is tender. Drain off the grease. Add ketchup, sugar, vinegar, mustard, celery seed, and Worcestershire sauce and simmer on low heat for 20 minutes. Stir to avoid sticking. When thoroughly cooked, remove from stove and place in a serving dish or storage container. Use for spicy Sloppy Joes or as a delicious Coney Sauce

Welcome Home Family Dining

Bryan, OH

136 North Main Street
Bryan, OH 43506
(419) 636-1365

Welcome Home was a welcomed sight as I cruised into Bryan, a small town in northwestern Ohio, population of 8,545 according to the 2010 Census. This is not a fancy diner, but the food is hardy and made from scratch. It's the kind that sticks to your ribs. They also serve a rich blend of pick-me-up coffee along with their specialty: Betty's Chocolate Cake.

Now, Chef Betty Speiser has been making this delicacy longer than she can remember, and it is to "die for," as they say. After helping myself to a generous serving, I agreed that it is the best in the area. In order to assuage my guilt in eating dessert first, I tried another specialty, the Kentucky Hash with a couple of eggs, prepared over-easy or "sunnyside up," as my father would say. Excellent ... just like being at home. And everyone is welcome!

Made In The Pan Chocolate Cake

3 cups white flour
2 cups white sugar
1 teaspoon baking soda
½ teaspoon salt, optional
5 tablespoons cocoa
2 tablespoons vinegar
1 cup cold water
1 teaspoon real vanilla
Chocolate icing, homemade or commerical

Preheat oven to 350 degrees. In a greased 9 x 13 inch baking pan, mix all dry ingredients (flour, sugar, baking soda, salt, and cocoa) together. Add vinegar, water and vanilla. Mix thoroughly until smooth. Bake for 40 minutes until a toothpick inserted in the middle of the cake comes out dry. Allow to cool before frosting with chocolate icing. Decorate as you wish.

Kentucky Hash

4 to 5 fried or shredded "tators," peeled and sliced
½ cup onion, diced
½ cup green pepper, diced
⅓ cup diced sausage, ham, bacon bits or other choice of meat
½ cup Colby Jack cheese, shredded
4 to 6 eggs, scrambled or over easy

Hash can be served two ways: as a side to complement eggs or in a baked egg casserole. Basically, the preparation of the hash is the same. The following is the recipe for the casserole.

Preheat oven to 350 degrees. Layer raw tators on the bottom of a greased oven-proof roasting pan. Then add onion, green pepper and meat. Top with eggs of your choice and finish with a layer of cheese. Bake until eggs are done and tators are soft.

NORTH EAST
REGION

356 Fighter Group North Canton, OH

Ashland-Wooster Drive-In Ashland, OH

CW Bergerstein's Great Sandwich Works Wooster, OH

Doc's Deli Mansfield, OH

Melvin's Brick Oven and Bakery Wooster, OH

Mohican Tavern Loudonville, OH

Pickle Bills Grand River, OH

Spat's Café Mentor, OH

TJ's Restaurant Wooster, OH

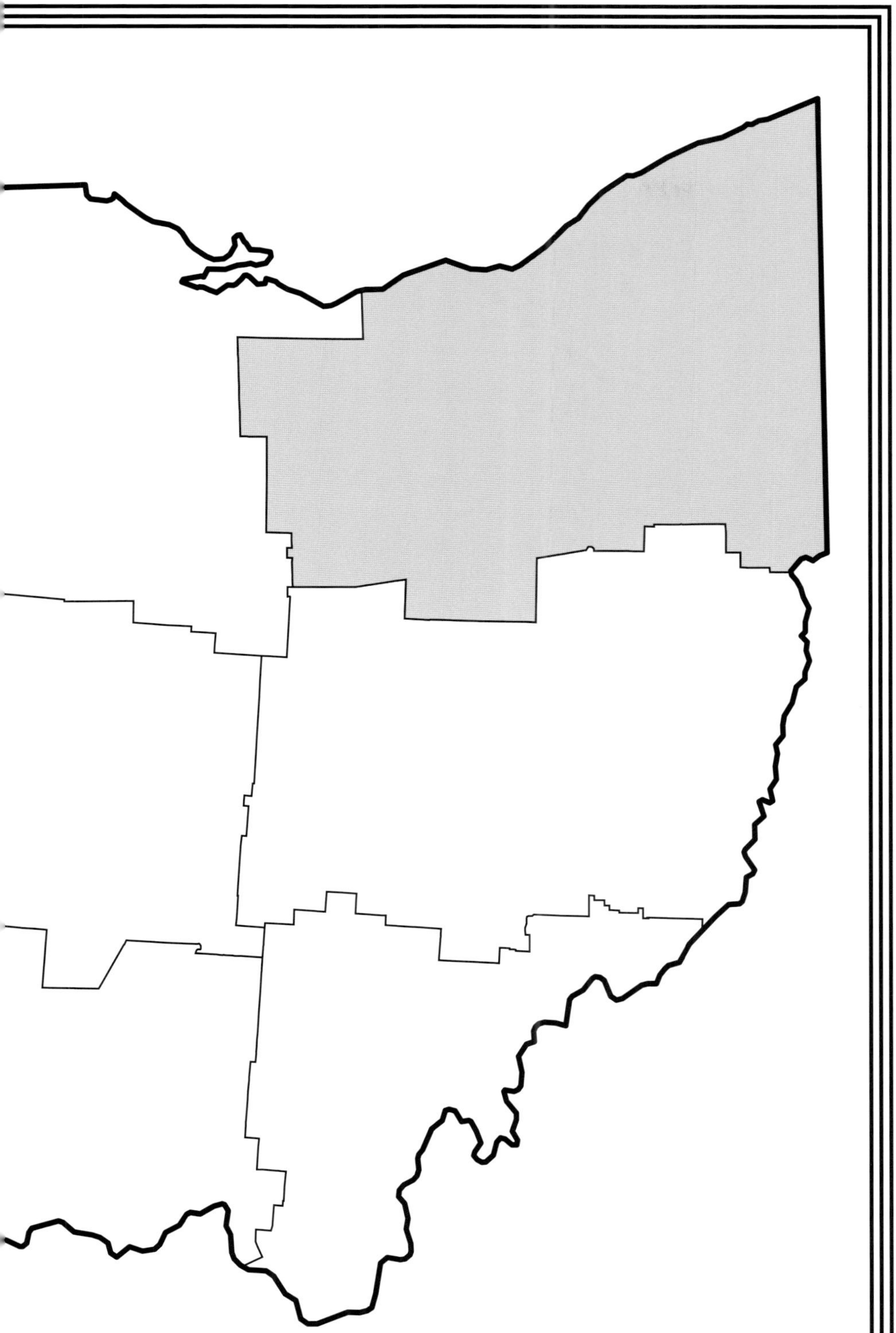

356 Fighter Group

North Canton, OH

4919 Mount Pleasant Road
North Canton, OH 44720
(330) 494-3500
www.356fg.com

This World War II theme restaurant, located on the edge of the North Canton airport, has been in business for more than 25 years. I found it captivating with war memorabilia everywhere, both inside and outside, and packed on both floors of the restaurant. It took me back to the memories of my father's war stories which I depicted in my book, *Allies Forever: The Life and Times of an American Prisoner of War* (Outskirts Press, 2009). The music in the background and pictures of that era, touched my heart as I enjoyed the fine cuisine that would make any soldier proud. Owner Bob Scofield gave me a tour of the place providing me with the story behind the numerous acquisitions he has collected over the years.

He also shared the following recipe which is one of the restaurant's originals and one of their most popular dishes. It has certainly stood the test of time and continues to be a favorite. God bless our troops; they would love to eat here!

Farmhouse Chicken

Marinade

1 tablespoon Lawry's Seasoning
1 tablespoon garlic, minced
3 cups salad oil
1 tablespoon ground coarse black pepper
1 ounce lemon juice
½ cup white wine
1 tablespoon rosemary
1 tablespoon paprika
8 ounce breast of chicken, thawed

Mix together Lawry's Seasoning, garlic, oil, black pepper, lemon juice, wine, rosemary and paprika. Whisk until these ingredients are blended together.

Place chicken breast in a pan and cover with marinade. Soak in the marinade overnight. When the meat is removed from the liquid it should be thoroughly coated. Shake any excess marinade off before grilling.

Grilled Chicken
1 ounce Virginia ham, sliced thin
2 ounces of Jack cheese, sliced
2 ounces mushrooms, sliced and sautéed in butter

To capture the full taste, the chicken breast should be char-grilled with the skin side down. (Or the skin can be removed before grilling.) Cook the chicken until it is about 60% done before turning it over. If the skin is still present, remove it at this point and finish cooking without the skin. Before serving, cover the chicken with the thin slice of Virginia ham and top with the slices of the Jack cheese. Melt in an oven or under the lid of the grill. Add sautéed mushrooms for an eye appealing and delicious dish.

This is one serving and should be adjusted to accommodate the number of diners.

NORTH EAST

Ashland-Wooster Drive-In

Ashland, OH

1134 East Main Street
Ashland, OH 44805
(419) 281-2658
www.ashland-wooster.com

Some of us are old enough to remember the drive-in restaurants of yesteryear where you stayed in the car and the server came out, sometimes on roller skates, and took your order. A few minutes later she would deliver it on a tray that attached to the car window. I thought those days were over until I found this original drive-in located in Ashland.

It brought back some great memories of neighborhood kids piling into our wood-paneled station wagon and stopping to eat at the drive-in restaurant on our way to the drive-in theater where we watched the latest movies.

Great memories of bygone days can be relived, at least partially, at this drive-in that is located on the right side of East Main Street as you drive into Ashland. It's a lot of fun especially for the kids!

Hot Pepper Butter

40 or 41 peppers, any kind (include hot ones), chopped
1 onion
6 cups sugar
1 quart mustard
1 quart vinegar
1 cup flour
1 tablespoon salt

Blend the peppers and onion in a food processor until pureed. Pour into a large pot and add sugar, mustard, vinegar, flour and salt. Bring the mixture to a boil on medium heat. Keep stirring until blended well. Pour into clean hot pint jars, wipe off mouth of the jar, seal and place upside down for 24 hours. Makes 10 to 11 pints. This pepper butter is good on and with most everything that needs a little extra kick. It also makes a nice homemade Christmas gift when wrapped up with a big bow.

Boy Scout Stew

½ pound ground beef
2 to 3 white potatoes, sliced
1 to 2 onions, sliced
6 small package fresh mushrooms
1 small bag frozen peas
1 small bag frozen carrots
Salt and pepper
Seasoning salt
Garlic powder
1 can cream of mushroom soup

In a large piece of heavy duty foil, combine ground beef, potatoes, onions, mushrooms, peas, and carrots. Add salt, pepper, seasoning salt and garlic powder to taste. Pour ½ of the can of soup over the mixture. Tightly wrap the foil and place the package on hot coals for 25 to 30 minutes. Or place on gas grill for 40 minutes (20 minutes per side). Remove from the foil and serve. Makes 2 servings.

NORTH EAST

CW Bergerstein's Great Sandwich Works

Wooster, OH

359 West Liberty Street
Wooster, OH 44691
(330) 264-6263
www.tjsrestaurants.com/cws.htm

If you are travelling through Wooster for any reason, you have got to visit this unique set of restaurants: Bergerstein's, Melvin's and TJ's. All are located in the same building.

Bergerstein's is open in the afternoons and evenings, and specializes in wings, burgers, and quick foods among other items. Along with Bergerstein's, Melvin's and TJ's each has its own menu, specials and atmosphere. Get more detailed information about all of them from their listings in the North Eastern Region of my *Eating Your Way Across Ohio* book.

Bergerstein's highly visible motto is: "The place to meet, eat, and share good times." And from what I saw on a Friday night, that was true. The place was packed!

Dagwood Burger

2 8-ounce beef patties
1 slice American cheese
1 slice Swiss cheese
2 strips of bacon, cooked
1 ounce banana peppers
1 ounce chili sauce
1 slice of red onion
2 slices salami
1 slice Provolone cheese
Lettuce
1 Kaiser bun

This is a house favorite. Grill burger patties to desired temperature (rare to well done). On one patty add the American and Swiss cheese, bacon & banana peppers. On other patty add chili sauce, red onion, salami, and Provolone cheese. Stack patties on the Kaiser bun to make one sandwich. Add lettuce and a toothpick through the top of a Kaiser bun in order to hold the sandwich together. The chef dares you to finish!

Balsalmic Chicken

Balsamic Vinaigrette
1 chicken breast
Asiago cheese

This is one of Bergerstein's best selling entrees. Marinate the chicken breast for 15 minutes in your favorite Balsamic Vinaigrette. Grill to perfection and finish by melting Asiago cheese on top. Serve with your favorite seasonal vegetable and Garlic Spinach Rice. (See below)

Garlic Spinach Rice

Since the chef did not provide me with the Garlic Spinach Rice recipe mentioned above, I have added one of my favorite recipes to complement Bergerstein's Balsamic Chicken dish. Give it a try!

1 10-ounce package frozen spinach, chopped
1 cup water
1 tablespoon garlic, minced
½ cup onion, chopped
2 tablespoons olive oil
2 cups rice, long grain or brown
Seasoning salt

Thaw and drain spinach and combine with water, garlic and onion. Puree mixture in a blender until smooth, and set it aside. In a large pan, heat oil over medium heat and add rice stirring until the oil and rice are blended. Slowly pour spinach mixture over rice and mix well. Over high heat bring to a boil then immediately reduce heat to low, cover and simmer until no liquid appears in the pan and the rice is tender, about 10 minutes. Salt to taste.

NORTH EAST

Doc's Deli

Mansfield, OH

424 Glessner Avenue
Mansfield, OH 44903
(419) 775-7775
www.docsdelimansfield.com

This is a neat little place located in downtown Mansfield about a block away from a unique old fashioned outdoor carousel. (Really! Check it out.) Doc's reminded me of a smaller version of a New York deli where you can order a Pastrami and Rye, Corned Beef Panini, Ham and Cheese or Cream of Broccoli or Potato Soup. All breads, meats and cheeses are fresh and the soups are homemade. You can either order from the menu or the placard on the wall, and then watch your meal being made, just like in New York.

Another interesting feature about Doc's is that you can build your favorite sandwich creation and owner Susan Vander Maas will store it in a database so that you can have the same sandwich when you come back. I think that's real customer service!!

Susan has been in business since 2007 and has created a niche in this town. Much of her business comes from the local hospital about a block away, but she gets a fair amount of tourist traffic too. I enjoyed my visit to this pristine deli and found the food to be both tasty and nutritious with plenty of fresh chopped veggies.

Baba Ghannouj

1 small eggplant, peeled
½ cup Tahini (sesame paste)
2 tablespoons olive oil
8 tablespoons lemon juice
2 teaspoons garlic, minced
Pinch of salt
Water as needed

Cube and mix eggplant with Tahini and olive oil. Grill until tender, but not mushy. Combine cooled eggplant, lemon juice, garlic and salt in a food processor and blend until smooth. Store in a glass container in the refrigerator. Use as a healthy condiment for sandwiches in place of mayonnaise.

Doc's Deli Potato Soup

½ pound butter (2 sticks)
2 cups flour
48 ounces chicken broth
8 cups milk
8 potatoes, peeled, cubed & boiled
½ cup Cheddar cheese, shredded
½ cup Bacon Bits
2 tablespoons sugar
½ teaspoon garlic powder
½ teaspoon onion powder
2 tablespoons parsley

Make a rue by melting butter over a low heat and whisking in flour until it is absorbed by the butter and becomes like a paste. Slowly pour in chicken broth, whisking constantly to thin out the rue. When the rue and broth are mixed slowly add milk and the potatoes. Let this mixture heat to 120 degrees, stirring occasionally so it doesn't burn. Mix in shredded Cheddar cheese (more can be used if desired). After the cheese melts add Bacon Bits, sugar, garlic powder, onion powder, and parsley. Adjust the spices to taste.

Melvin's Brick Oven & Bakery

Wooster, OH

359 West Liberty Street
Wooster, OH 44691
(330) 264-6263
www.tjsrestaurants.com/cws.htm

Melvin's is the second establishment in the Wooster restaurant trilogy along with CW Burgerstein's and TJ's. This one location houses these three different restaurants with three distinctive menus. Each of the restaurants has its own specialties designed to offer the hungry traveler, adventuresome spirit or discerning diner something different at one location.

Melvin's features a wood-burning brick oven where fresh baked breads, gourmet pizzas and paninis are prepared under the watchful eye of the guests. A variety of fresh salads and homemade soups is offered in a casual setting that combines the laid back style of Burgerstein's with the sophistication of TJ's.

In addition to the freshly baked goods, Melvin's menu also has an international flair. The chef combines herbs, spices and other seasonings to create unique flavors in distinctive dishes like Grecian Chicken, Italian Sirloin Steak and Thai Walnut Grouper. There are so many excellent selections and so little time to try them all, you will want to visit time and time again! The following recipes are a good start and they give a taste of the chef's creativity at work.

Baked Acorn Squash

1 acorn squash
¼ cup olive oil
½ cup water
Salt and pepper to taste
1 red onion
1 zucchini
1 yellow squash
¼ cup your favorite Balsamic dressing
½ cup Provolone cheese, shredded
Seasonal vegetables

Prepare the acorn squash by slicing it in half, and scraping out and discarding the seeds. Place on a cookie sheet or in a shallow pan. Brush with oil and add water equally to both sides of the squash. Salt and pepper to taste then oven or wood fire roast until tender but not falling apart. At 350 degrees, this will usually take about 20 minutes

Julianne the onion, zucchini and yellow squash, and sauté with the remaining olive oil. Salt and pepper to taste. Set aside and chill in the fridge. Most any seasonal vegetable or combination can be used depending on your taste. Stuff acorn with the chilled sautéed vegetables. Drizzle with your favorite Balsamic dressing and top with shredded Provolone cheese. Oven bake or wood fire at 400 degrees for about 15 minutes or until the cheese is golden brown. This is a great seasonal and vegetarian dish. Serves 2.

NORTH EAST

P. E. Island Mussels
(Prince Edward)

1 tablespoon olive oil
1 garlic clove, minced
1 pound P.E. Island mussels
1/3 cup white cooking wine
2 lemon wedges
1 teaspoon oregano, dry
1 tablespoon pesto
1 teaspoon butter
1 tablespoon heavy cream

Heat olive oil in medium sized saucepan. Sauté garlic until tender and stir in mussels and white wine. Wait until the wine is simmering then add lemon wedges, oregano, pesto, butter and slowly stir in heavy cream. Simmer over low heat until mussels are cooked thoroughly and opened. Serve with your favorite bread.

MELVIN'S
Brick Oven and Bakery

Mohican Tavern

Loudonville, OH

267 West Main Street
Loudonville, OH 44842
(419) 994-0079
www.mohicantavern.com

This sleepy little town is just a few miles from Mohican State Park which is located in the Mohican-Memorial State Forest. In the summer when tourist traffic picks up, the sleepy town wipes its eyes and wakes up to accommodate the deluge of hikers, bikers and day-trippers invading the territory. Of course, wherever there is a crowd there is a need for food and the Mohican Tavern is ready to provide a versatile selection of Grilled Chicken, Chicken Pasta, Walleye, Pork Chops, Potato Pierogies, and Surf & Turf (New York strip steak and crab cakes).

I discovered that this was one of the few places in the area east of Interstate 71 to enjoy a wholesome sit down meal in a family atmosphere. Even though there is a full bar in the main dining room, there are plenty of tables located far enough away from the bar to accommodate children of all ages.

Of the many places I have reviewed in Ohio, this is one that I want to visit again. Not only is the restaurant a draw, but the Mohican Forest and State Park located nearby have so much to offer. I'm looking forward to returning to the area sometime soon.

Buffalo Chicken Wrap

2 chicken breasts, skinless, boneless
2 ounces adobo seasoning*
2 ounces olive oil

Preheat oven to 400 degrees. Mix the Adobo seasoning and olive oil in a bowl and coat the chicken thoroughly. Bake at 400 degrees for 40 to 50 minutes until juices run clear then finish by grilling the meat on each side for 1 to 2 minutes. Chop into small chunks and set aside.

(* Adobo seasoning is traditionally a dry spice mix sold commercially.)

Buffalo Ranch Sauce
2 ounces ranch dressing
2 ounces buffalo sauce*
1 teaspoon adobo seasoning
1 teaspoon western BBQ seasoning

Mix all ingredients together in a small bowl and set aside. (*Buffalo sauce is a hot sauce often used to coat chicken wings.)

Putting It All Together:
Tomato basil wraps
¼ cup leaf lettuce, washed and shredded
1 medium tomato, diced
1 red onion, diced
¼ cup Cheddar cheese
¼ cup dried hickory smoked bacon, diced

Place grilled chicken in the middle of a tomato basil wrap. Top with lettuce, tomatoes, onions, cheese, bacon and drizzle with homemade Buffalo Ranch Sauce. Roll the wrap up tightly and insert one or two toothpicks to hold it together. Fry in an oiled pan for 1 to 2 minutes in order to melt the cheese and heat the wrap. Don't overcook.

Baked Tilapia

8 ounces fresh Tilapia
1 cup sea salt
2 ounces garlic powder
2 ounces coarse ground black pepper
2 ounces minced onions
3 tablespoons butter

Preheat oven to 350 degrees. Season the Tilapia with salt, garlic, and pepper. Pan sear with onions in butter over medium heat for 2 to 3 minutes on each side then finish by baking for 10 minutes. Top with fresh salsa (see below).

Fresh Salsa:
4 medium tomatoes, diced
1 red onion, diced
2 ounces garlic, minced in oil
6 sprigs fresh cilantro
6 sprigs fresh basil
½ cup olive oil

Combine the tomatoes, onion, garlic, fresh herbs and toss with olive oil. Pour a generous amount on top of the baked Tilapia. Garnish with a sprig of parsley and serve

Pickle Bills

Grand River, OH

101 River Street
Grand River, OH 44045
(800) 352-6343
www.picklebills.com

Wow! What a crazy, zany and fun place. It would take a week to explore this expansive multi-tiered building in order to see the jumble of knick knacks, ornaments, decorations and bodies. Yes, bodies in the strangest places! Not real ones, of course, but mannequins dressed in dive suits and helmets, lingerie, and other outfits. I was fascinated by this stimulating atmosphere as I was led to a table in the main dining room. Once seated, I discovered that there are many dining areas with one along the water's edge and another on the second floor with a great view of Lake Erie.

When the server brought the menu, I found it to be chocked full of selections, including fresh water haddock, perch and walleye caught fresh daily. I visited the self-serve Oyster and Clam bar twice and ate my fill.

I discovered later that Pickle Bill's reputation for seafood excels over others in the area. So between the food and the atmosphere, Pickle Bill's is a one of a kind place.

Pickle Bill's Clam Chowder

1 46-ounce can of clam juice
3½ pounds potatoes, peeled and diced to 3/8 inch
4 cups chicken stock
2 bay leaves, whole
½ pound bacon, sliced 1 inch x 1 inch
1½ pounds Spanish onions, diced 3/8 inch
2 cups celery, diced 3/8 inch
¼ pound butter (1 stick)
3 ounces flour
1 quart + 1 cup milk
½ teaspoon white pepper
¼ tablespoon coarse black pepper
1 teaspoon thyme, dried leaf
1 cup heavy cream
2 51-ounce cans sea clams, chopped, not drained

Place clam juice, potatoes, chicken stock, and bay leaves in a stock pot. Cook until the potatoes are almost tender. Remove bay leaves. Meanwhile, sauté bacon until just crisp. Then add onions, celery and butter and sauté until the celery is soft, but not brown. Add flour to the vegetables and stir to combine completely and to thicken. Cook for 2 to 3 minutes. Slowly add potato mixture, which is the chowder broth. Stir thoroughly. Heat all the milk in a double boiler until temperature is above 100 degrees, and then combine with the chowder. Add all seasonings, and stir well. Add cream and clams, stir thoroughly and simmer for 20 minutes over low heat and serve. Yields 1½ gallons. Chowder can be stored in a glass container but should be consumed within a couple days.

Pickle Bill's Crab Cakes

¾ cup Hellmann's Mayonnaise
1 tablespoon Old Bay Seasoning
1 teaspoon cayenne pepper
1¼ teaspoons ground mustard
1½ tablespoons parsley
1½ tablespoons lemon juice
½ tablespoon Worcestershire Sauce
3 dashes Tabasco Sauce
3 eggs
1 cup chives
8 ounces potato chips, crushed
4½ pounds jumbo lump crab meat
1½ cups Panko bread crumbs

In a large bowl, add first 11 ingredients. Mix thoroughly. Fold in lump crab meat. Be careful not to mash up the crab pieces. If the mixture is too moist, add bread crumbs. Gently mix again. Form into 2-ounce patties and slowly brown over medium high heat. Serve with corn relish and mustard sauce (see below). Yields 50 2-ounce cakes that can easily be frozen and heated later.

White Corn Relish

3 cups sweet corn kernels, thawed and drained
6 ounces red bell peppers, ³/₈", diced
½ ounce cilantro, minced
¾ cup red onion, diced ³/₈"
¼ cup Balsamic vinegar
½ cup olive oil
½ teaspoon salt
1 teaspoon coarse ground black pepper

Mix all ingredients thoroughly and store in a glass container. Keep refrigerated.

Mustard Sauce

½ cup brown grainy mustard
½ cup Dijon mustard
½ cup honey

Mix all ingredients, place in a glass jar and keep refrigerated.

NORTH EAST

Spat's Cafe

Mentor, OH

9853 Johnnycakes-Ridge Road
Mentor, OH 44060
(440) 352-0597

This is a lovely and spacious café with seating on a covered porch as well as inside by the bar or in the large dining room. The term "café" is somewhat misleading in that it implies a small intimate restaurant with a limited menu, but that is not the case at Spat's. They offer the usual bar food, but they go beyond the "usual" and feature Sauteéd Pierogies, Eggplant Parmesan, and their specialty, Spaghetti and Meatballs. They also offer fried or broiled Lake Walleye and Steamed Mussels.

I sat in the bar area with owners Penny and Paul Gamrat and noticed that it was not a typical bar. There are a number of televisions that create the atmosphere of a sports bar, but the décor is less sporty and designed more for comfort. The covered porch was even cozy with baskets of fresh flowers hanging around the dining area.

Penny shared the following recipes as a delicious treat for my readers, especially her recipe for meatballs. And if you have ever hesitated to try to make Balsalmic Vinaigrette, here is an easy recipe.

Meatballs

10 pounds ground beef
10 pounds ground pork
2 cups chopped garlic
1 cup parsley
1 cup oregano
1 cup basil
4 cups Parmesan cheese
8 cups of bread crumbs
1 quart Egg Beaters
1 quart heavy cream

Mix all ingredients together using the paddle attachment of the mixer or fold the ingredients together by hand. Be careful not to over mix. Use a small scoop or small spoon to form balls and place on a cookie sheet about half an inch apart. Cook at 325 degrees for 1 hour until the internal temperature reaches 165 degrees. Use the meatballs in spaghetti recipes or by themselves in barbeque sauce.

Balsalmic Vinaigrette

1 24-ounce jar Grey Poupon mustard
4 cups honey
1 cup chopped garlic
½ cup salt
½ cup pepper
1 gallon Balsamic vinegar
1 gallon blended oil

In a large bowl using a wire whip of the mixer combine the mustard, honey, chopped garlic, salt, pepper and vinegar. Mix thoroughly on medium speed for 5 minutes. Then slowly add the oil. Mix again and store in a glass container. Makes 2 gallons.

TJ's Restaurant

Wooster, OH

359 West Liberty Street
Wooster, OH 44691
(330) 264-6263
www.tjsrestaurants.com/cws.htm

TJ's is the third establishment in the Wooster three-in-one restaurant trilogy, along with CW Burgerstein's and Melvin's. As mentioned earlier, each of these restaurants has its own specialties; however, TJ's is more upscale and features specials like Creamy Lobster and Asparagus Angel Hair Pasta, Blackened Grouper with Louisiana Shrimp Sauce, and Sauteed Halibut. Chef Glenn Meier has created dishes to offer something that the diner may not find elsewhere, even at the adjoining establishments.

The atmosphere and the restaurant's décor are also more stylish than the other two, which is reflected in the prices. All in all, this three-in-one idea not only provides a variety of food choices, but it caters to many different tastes and accommodates three times the number of visitors that a single restaurant might offer. No matter which dining experience you choose, you can bring the whole family.

Cajun Shrimp & Sausage Fettuccine

1 tablespoon olive oil
4 jumbo shrimp, uncooked, tail off
5 ounces cooked spicy Italian sausage
1 ounce tomatoes, diced
1 teaspoon fresh garlic, minced
1 ounce button mushrooms, sliced
1 ounce pickled yellow peppers
¼ cup white table wine
⅓ cup heavy cream
1 tablespoon Cajun seasoning
8 ounces fettuccine pasta, cooked and oiled
Salt and pepper
1 ounce Asiago cheese

Heat olive oil in medium skillet and sauté shrimp, sausage, tomatoes, garlic, mushrooms, and yellow peppers. De-glaze with the white wine, mixing well, in order to make a thin sauce. Then blend in heavy cream and Cajun seasoning. Stir thoroughly. Reduce the heat and add the fettuccine pasta. Cook until hot throughout and slightly thickened. Adjust salt and pepper to desired taste. Serve in your favorite bowl and garnish with the Asiago cheese.

Tomato Bruschetta

2 slices Focaccia bread
2 tablespoons olive oil
2 ounces fresh Mozzarella cheese
2 Roma tomatoes diced
1 tablespoon basil pesto
¼ cup Balsamic Vinaigrette
Asiago cheese

This is a simple but delicious item on the menu. Place 2 slices of Focaccia bread on a flat top grill or heated large skillet. Add olive oil and cook both sides of the bread until golden brown. Melt the cheese equally on both pieces of the bread. In another bowl, combine tomatoes, pesto and Balsamic Vinaigrette. Pour over both slices of bread and garnish with Asiago cheese. This makes a delicious and light summer time dish.

TJ's
RESTAURANT
Since 1964
Fine Dining

CENTRAL WEST REGION

Bel Lago Waterfront Dining Westerville, OH

Ben & Joy's Mt. Sterling, OH

Bistro Off Broadway Greenville, OH

Chattan Loch Bellefontaine, OH

Cherry Street Diner Ashville, OH

Goodwin's Family Restaurant Circleville, OH

JR Hooks Café Circleville, OH

La Palma Mexican Restaurant Bellefontaine, OH

Oscar's Washington Court House, OH

Peach's Grill Yellow Springs, OH

The Purple Turtle Café Washington Court House, OH

The Refectory Columbus, OH

Tuscan Table Circleville, OH

Werner's Smoke House Jeffersonville, OH

Young's Jersey Dairy Yellow Springs, OH

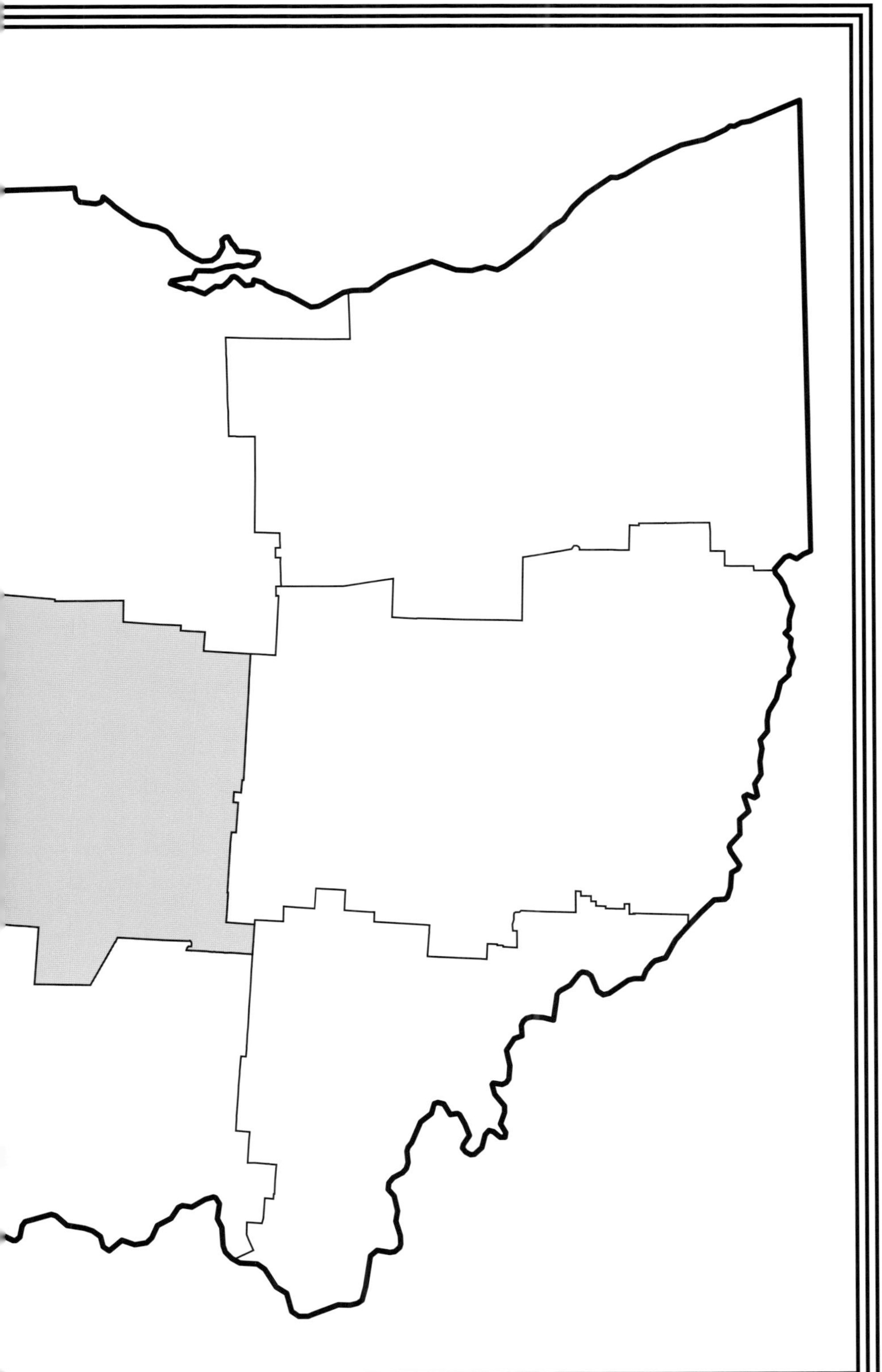

Bel Lago Waterfront Dining

Westerville, OH

170 N. Sunbury Road
Westerville, OH 43081
(614) 891-0200
www.bellagobistro.com

I included only a few 5-star restaurants in my *Eating Your Way Across Ohio* book and this is one of the best. Located on the shore of Hoover Reservoir, it is what I envisioned when I lived in this area years ago before any commercial property was developed, I thought the waterfront would be the perfect setting for either casual or more elegant dining and, as it turns out, I was right. Bel Lago captures the elegant scene, but it also provides a fun and friendly atmosphere.

The distinctive design of the building utilizes nature as a backdrop, and from almost every interior angle there is a view of the water. The restaurant is designed with a classic Italian flair highlighted with a magnificent canopied bar, and in the winter there is a warm fire burning in the massive stone fireplace. This is a lovely place to dine all year round.

The quality of the cuisine matches the tastefulness of the décor and provides many Italian specialties accented with a variety of American entrees, including Mac and Cheese which I found to be both delicate and delicious.

Lobster Mac and Cheese

2 pounds pipette pasta, uncooked
2 tablespoons real butter
2 tablespoons garlic, minced
12 ounces lobster meat, claw and knuckle
4 ounces white wine
2 quarts of cream, we suggest heavy cream
36 ounces Cheddar and Mozzarella mixed
6 ounces Tabasco Bloody Mary Mix

Cook the pasta in boiling water until al dente* and then rinse in cold water, drain, refrigerate and, finally, let the pasta rest. Melt the butter in a sauce pan over low heat. Once completely melted, add garlic and sauté over low heat. When the garlic is soft, add the lobster and sauté briefly until the meat is warm throughout. Add white wine to the pan and simmer over low heat until the smell of alcohol has vanished. Add heavy cream and reduce over low heat until it slightly thickens. Then add chilled pasta to the pan and continue to cook over low heat until the mixture begins to simmer, at which time, add the cheese. Once the cheese has melted, mix in salt and pepper to taste. Add 1 ounce of warm Bloody Mary Mix to each serving dish. This recipe serves 6 people generously.

(* Al dente refers to the resistance of the pasta when cooked. It should be slightly firm but not tough.)

Ben & Joy's

Mt. Sterling, OH

35 South London Street
Mt. Sterling, OH 43143
(740) 869-4324

Mt. Sterling is a traditional American small town and one of the many charming villages scattered throughout Ohio where there is usually one carry out, one small grocery store and a gas station. But this town also has Ben & Joy's eatery located on a corner in the middle of town. The restaurant entertains a brisk business drawing from local companies, residents and travelers on their way to work or to nearby Deer Creek for a day of swimming, fishing or boating.

A unique part of the restaurant is Joy's Angel Room that contains hundreds of angel figurines of all sizes that make great gifts or keepsakes to remember your travels through small town America. Everyone needs a guardian angel.

After Ben passed away, Joy's dedication to her customers motivated her to keep the place open with the help of family and friends. She continues to provide fresh ingredients, many from local farmers' markets, in her made-from-scratch dishes found either on the menu or on the buffet. Following are a couple of her all time favorite dishes.

Pickled Beets

1 quart vinegar
1 quart sugar
2 quarts beets, drained and sliced
1 large onion, sliced thin

This is a simple, yet delicious recipe for making this picnic favorite. Heat the vinegar and sugar in a saucepan and bring to a gentle boil. Stir constantly until the sugar has dissolved. Cut beets in 2 to 2½ inch slices and place them with the onions in a heavy flat bottom ceramic bowl. Remove the vinegar and sugar mix from the stove and pour over the beets and onions to cover. Cool on countertop then refrigerate overnight. Store in a glass container in the refrigerator.

Pistachio Salad

4 11-ounce cans of pineapple tidbits
4 3.5-ounce boxes of pistachio pudding
1 16-ounce bag of miniature marshmallows
1 pound of whipped topping or Cool Whip

Mix the juice from the pineapple tidbits with the pudding until the mixture is smooth. Fold the pineapple and marshmallows into the pudding mix until evenly distributed and top with whipped topping before serving.

Bistro Off Broadway

Greenville, OH

117 East Fifth Street
Greenville, OH 45331
(937) 316-5000
www.thebistrooffbroadway.com

The term "eye-candy" comes to mind in describing the décor of the Bistro Off Broadway. Vintage toy cars and planes hang from the ceiling with old fashioned neon lights providing much of the interior lighting. Booths are set up against the walls and tables occupy the main floor. This is a fun family place with a menu that provides something for everyone. I had the spicy Amber Bock cheese dip served with soft pretzel bites and the crab cakes with remoulade sauce which were quite tasty, but the menu offers a number of other tempting dishes.

The Bistro's Beer Cheese Dip

½ pound white American cheese
½ pound Monterey Jack cheese
½ cup milk
½ cup Amber Bock beer
½ tablespoon Worcestershire sauce
½ tablespoon dry mustard
1 teaspoon Dijon mustard
½ teaspoon Tabasco sauce
¼ teaspoon cayenne pepper

Cut white American cheese and Monterey Jack cheese into small pieces. Place in the top portion of the double boiler along with the milk. Heat until the cheese is melted. Mix well with a wire whip. Place the beer, Worcestershire sauce, dry mustard, Dijon mustard, Tabasco and pepper in a small mixing bowl. Mix until completely blended. Add to the melted cheese and stir with a wire whip. Remove from the heat and serve with soft pretzels, tortilla chips or French fries. Makes approximately 3½ cups.

Blackened Mahi Mahi with Peach Salsa

Seasoning
1½ teaspoons ground cumin
1 teaspoon garlic powder
1 teaspoon dried oregano
½ teaspoon ground ginger
½ teaspoon smoked paprika
½ teaspoon kosher salt
½ teaspoon ground black pepper
¼ teaspoon cayenne pepper

Combine all of the seasoning ingredients in a small bowl. Mix well and set aside.

Peach Salsa
14 ounces tomatoes, chopped
14 ounces peaches, chopped
1 jalapeno pepper, seeded and chopped
½ cup red onion, chopped
2 tablespoons fresh cilantro, chopped
1 teaspoon cumin, ground
1 teaspoon garlic, minced
1 lime, juiced

Make the Peach Salsa by combining all ingredients in another bowl and mixing well. Set this aside.

4 4-ounce Mahi Mahi fillets
Olive oil

Lightly oil the fillets and sprinkle them with the seasoning. Preheat the grill to medium high heat. Cook fillets 3 to 4 minutes per side or until desired doneness. When they are easy to flake with a fork remove from the grill. Serve with the Peach Salsa. Yields 4 servings.

Pina Colada Cake with Coconut Cream Cheese Frosting

1 cup (2 sticks) butter, room temperature
2 cups sugar
4 eggs
3 cups self-rising flour
1 cup Pina Colada mix
1 teaspoon vanilla extract

Preheat oven to 350 degrees. Grease and flour 3 round 9-inch cake pans. Cream butter until fluffy using an electric mixer. Add sugar and continue to cream well for 6 to 8 minutes. Add eggs, one at a time, beating well after each addition. Add flour and milk alternately to creamed mixture, beginning and ending with flour. Then add the Pina Colada mix, and vanilla. Continue to beat until just barely mixed. Divide batter equally among prepared pans. Level batter in each pan by holding the pan 3 or 4 inches above counter, then drop it flat onto the counter. Do this several times to release air bubbles and assure a level cake.

Bake for 25 to 30 minutes or until a toothpick inserted into the middle comes out dry. Cool in pans for 5 to 10 minutes. Then invert cakes onto cooling racks. After each is cooled completely, spread each cake layer with your favorite frosting or Coconut Cream Cheese Frosting (see below). Carefully stack to make a 3-layer cake.

Coconut Cream Cheese Frosting
8 ounce Philadelphia cream cheese, softened
½ cup (1 stick) butter, softened
2 pounds powdered sugar
4 tablespoons milk
1 teaspoon vanilla extract
1 cup coconut, toasted

Beat cream cheese and butter in a large bowl with electric mixer on medium speed until light and fluffy. Add sugar alternately with the milk, beating until well blended after each addition. Add vanilla and mix well. At this point, add the toasted coconut and spread on each layer of the cake. Pat the coconut around the sides of the cake after stacked and iced. Yields approximately 5 cups.

The
Bistro
OFF BROADWAY
OPEN

K-STATE

Chattan Loch

Bellefontaine, OH

212 East Columbus Avenue
Bellefontaine, OH 43311
(937) 592-2696

Owner Terry McPherson has changed the focus of her restaurant, from day-to-day food service to a catering and banquet facility. She is able to cater up to 300 guests on or off site with five course meals or box lunch options. But she still maintains her mission to employ those with developmental disabilities in order to acclimate them to a work environment where they can learn new skills. Terry has also included a retail market by offering her canned "house-made" vinaigrettes, sauces, and salsas for sale. In addition, she provides a "Meal on the Go" plan where folks can order meals up to a week in advance, pick them up and serve at home.

Homemade Buttermilk Dressing

1 cup buttermilk
¼ cup sour cream
1 large clove garlic, grated or minced
1 tablespoon lemon juice
1 teaspoon hot sauce
3 tablespoons chives, finely chopped
1 tablespoon dill, finely chopped
Salt and pepper

Combine buttermilk with the sour cream, garlic, lemon juice, hot sauce, chives, and dill in a bowl and mix thoroughly. Salt and pepper to taste.

Garlic Roasted Potatoes

3 pounds main crop potatoes
⅓ cup regular olive oil
1 garlic head
Kosher salt

Preheat oven to 425 degrees. Wash, dry, peel and cut the potatoes into about ¾ inch squares. Lay potato pieces on a large oven tray and pour the oil over them and mix well. Separate the head of garlic into cloves adding them to the tray. Roast both potatoes and garlic for about 1 hour turning once or twice during that time until the potatoes are crispy and golden, but still soft on the inside. When they're done, remove to a large plate and sprinkle with salt. Serve immediately

Chocolate Peppermint Pattie Cake

To start, place 1 cup of Peppermint Pattie candies in the freezer for ease in cutting

Cake:
1 cup (2 sticks) butter
1 cup flour
14 ounces semisweet chocolate, chopped
¼ cup plus 2 tablespoons cream
6 eggs, separated
1 cup sugar
½ teaspoon kosher salt
2 teaspoons vanilla
1 cup Peppermint Pattie candies, diced into small pieces

Making the cake:
Preheat oven to 350 degrees. Butter a 9½ to 10-inch spring form pan and line the bottom with parchment paper. Lightly spread softened butter over the paper, and dust the paper with flour by tapping out the excess flour. In a saucepan, melt the chocolate with the butter and cream in the top of a double boiler. Set aside and let cool.

In the bowl of a mixer with a whip, beat the egg yolks with the sugar until very thick and light (about 5 minutes). Add the melted chocolate mixture to the egg yolks and mix until just blended. Add the remaining flour, salt, and vanilla. Mix until thoroughly combined, scraping the bowl once or twice. Transfer the batter to a large mixing bowl and stir in the Peppermint Pattie pieces. The mixture will be quite thick.

In a clean mixing bowl, with a clean whip, beat the egg whites to medium soft peaks. Lighten the cake batter by folding in one third of the beaten egg whites then gently mix in the remaining whites. Place the cake batter mixture in the prepared pan. Bake for approximately 45 to 50 minutes. When the top of the cake feels set and very fine hairline cracks just start to form around the edges, remove and cool in the pan on a rack.

Ganache Topping
1 cup cream
8 ounces semisweet chocolate, finely chopped

Heat the cream in a heavy bottomed saucepan to just under a boil. Add the chopped chocolate and, over very low heat, constantly stir the mixture. Cook until it is completely smooth. Strain through a fine sieve into a bowl and cool, stirring occasionally, until thickened and spreadable. This can take several hours. You can make the topping up to 3 days ahead, refrigerate it, and allow it to come to room temperature for several hours before using. You can also hasten the cooling process by placing the melted Ganache over an ice bath and gently stirring it until thickened; however, the resulting texture may not be quite as smooth and creamy.

Place the cooled cake upside down on a cardboard cake circle or a plate. Remove the sides and bottom of the spring form pan. Remove the parchment liner. Using an offset spatula, carefully spread the Ganache over what is now the top of the cake, drawing the Ganache all the way out to the edges of the cake. Using the offset spatula, level the edges to give the cake a finished look.

Cocoa Fudge Sauce:
8 tablespoons butter
½ cup brown sugar
⅓ cup unsweetened cocoa, sifted
1 cup cream
A few grains kosher salt
½ teaspoon vanilla extract

Melt the butter in a medium sized saucepan. Whisk in the sugar and cocoa and then whisk in the cream and salt. Bring to a simmer over medium low heat, whisking often. Allow to simmer for 8 to 10 minutes until the sauce has thickened somewhat. Remove from heat, add the vanilla and strain though a fine sieve to remove any lumps. Cool and serve at room temperature. This can be made up to 1 week ahead of time and it can also be frozen. Yields 2 cups.

Mint Syrup:
1¼ cups sugar
¾ cup water
2 cups packed fresh mint leaves

Combine the sugar and water in a small saucepan and bring to a boil over medium heat. Turn the heat down and simmer several minutes, until the sugar is completely dissolved and resembles a syrup consistency. Remove from heat and cool completely. Reserve.

Bring a small saucepan of water to a boil. Have a strainer and a bowl of ice water ready. Working quickly, place the mint leaves in the boiling water and blanch until just wilted (about 10 seconds). Immediately strain the mint and place the leaves directly in the ice water to set their color. Strain the mint again, pressing to remove excess liquid.

Place the mint leaves and half of the reserved syrup in a blender. Puree the mint, stopping several times to scrape down the blender bowl. Add the remaining syrup and blend for 2 minutes. Transfer the mixture to a clean storage container and allow it to sit overnight, covered, at room temperature. Strain the syrup through a fine mesh strainer and discard the solid mint puree. Store the syrup in the refrigerator for up to 2 weeks. Shake or stir lightly before using.

Use a hot, dry long-bladed knife to cut perfectly clean slices of the cake. Serve cake with whipped cream, cocoa fudge sauce, and a drizzle of mint syrup.

Cherry Street Diner

Ashville, OH

29 Cherry Street.
Ashville, OH 43103
(740) 983-9669

The distinctive white building on a side street in Ashville, about 20 minutes north of Circleville, is hard to miss once you find Cherry Street. When you see the large striped awning, you are there.

Breakfast begins to be served at 6 a.m. but don't count on dinner because they close at 2 p.m. Owner Pam Ward and her staff begin preparing food at 4 a.m. when most of us are still sleeping. I was impressed by her dedication in not only serving others so graciously, but in changing the menu and featuring specials that she knows her customers, especially her regulars, will enjoy. Call it good business sense, but she does know her clientele. If you are in the area, stop by for breakfast or a hardy homemade lunch. At the same time, enjoy the lighthearted and casual atmosphere where everyone knows everyone.

Meat Loaf

1½ pounds ground beef
½ cup dry bread crumbs
¼ cup onion, chopped
1½ teaspoons pepper
1½ teaspoons salt
1 egg, slightly beaten
½ cup milk
1½ cups ketchup

Set oven at 375 degrees. Lightly mix beef, bread crumbs, onion, pepper, salt, egg, milk and 1 cup ketchup. Form into a firm loaf and place in a greased pan. Bake for 1 hour. Remove from the oven and pour the remaining ketchup over the loaf. Bake 5 to 10 minutes longer.

Custard Pie

3 eggs
½ cup sugar
½ teaspoon salt
2¼ cups milk
1 teaspoon vanilla
Pie shell, unbaked

Set oven at 425 degrees. Beat eggs lightly. Gradually add sugar and salt, mix thoroughly and blend in milk and vanilla until smooth. Pour mixture into unbaked pie shell. Bake for 10 minutes, then reduce the temperature to 350 degrees and bake for an additional 25 to 30 minutes until the filling is firm. Let cool and serve.

Golden Brown Salmon Patties

2 cans salmon
1 medium onion, diced
2 eggs
1 cup saltines, crushed
⅓ cup cooking oil

Break up salmon in a bowl with a fork until it is flakey. Add onion and mix in eggs and saltines until all ingredients have blended together. Form individual fist-sized patties and fry either in a pan with 1/3 cup of cooking oil or in a deep fryer at 350 degrees until golden brown. Serve hot with your favorite cocktail or tartar sauce and garnish with a sprig of parsley.

CENTRAL WEST

Goodwin's Family Restaurant

Circleville, OH

214 Lancaster Pike, Route 22 East
Circleville, OH 43113
(740) 474-1238
www.goodwinsfamilyrestaurant.com

Art Goodwin has been serving up homemade comfort food in the Circleville area since 1979. Goodwin's daily buffet offers a wide variety of local favorites, but their most popular dish, and one that they are most famous for, is their broasted chicken. On average, they sell more than 2500 pieces per week which includes a brisk carry-out business. The recipe is a closely guarded family secret and one I think Art will take to his grave, which I hope is not soon.

Second to Goodwin's chicken are their onion rings which are a long standing tradition in town. Art was kind enough to share this recipe with me. Now you can make them at home, but remember, for the original taste, Goodwin's still makes the best. So when you are coming to Circleville for the Pumpkin Show, be sure to stop by their place for chicken, onion rings and so many other delicious items from the menu or on the daily buffet.

Homemade Onion Rings

Large Spanish onions, sliced about a ¼ inch thick
Milk, enough for dipping
Pillsbury flour, enough to form a batter
2 to 3 eggs, beaten
Lance cracker meal
Soybean oil to cover onion rings

The amount of each ingredient will depend on how many onions you are going to cook and how many servings you will need. Take care to follow each step carefully. Cut the onions to a thickness of ¼ inch and ring out or remove the core. Separate the rings and dip each in the milk then dip them in the flour. Let set up for 20 minutes so that the flour sticks firmly to the rings. Once the batter is firm, dip the rings in the egg and again in the milk wash. Finish by thoroughly covering the rings in the cracker meal. Once again, let the rings rest until the batter is firm then deep fry in soybean oil at 350 degrees for 2½ minutes. Serve with a favorite dipping sauce, like Ranch, Bleu cheese, or salsa.

J R Hooks Cafe

Circleville, OH

115 Watt Street
Circleville, OH 43113
(740) 474-2158
www.jrhooksrestaurant.com

Hooks is located in the heart of Circleville and has a long standing reputation for its fine cuisine. Though ownership has changed hands over the years, Hooks continues to provide award winning food and service. My husband and I have always enjoyed their Stuffed Mushrooms, but one of our special favorites is their Shrimp and Grits. An unusual combination for a northerner, but it works and it is delicious.

The menu offers something for everyone with New Orleans inspired American favorites like Cajun Meatloaf, Hunter Chicken, Apple Brandy Pork Chops and Beer Baked Ribs. We not only enjoy the cuisine, but also the pleasant and peaceful setting after a hectic day.

Chicken Stanley

1 9-ounce chicken breast

Marinade
1 cup white wine
6 cups Creole mustard

1 ounce drawn butter
1 ounce mushrooms, sliced
1 ounce zucchini, sliced
1 ounce red pepper, julienne
2 ounces mustard marinade
1 ounce cream

Mix the wine and mustard together and cover the chicken. Ideally refrigerate it overnight or at least for a few hours. Heat the butter in skillet being careful not to burn it. Add the marinated chicken breast and cook for 3 minutes until lightly browned. Add mushrooms, zucchini and red pepper, and cook for an additional 2 minutes until the chicken is cooked thoroughly and the vegetables are still firm. Stir in the mustard marinade and cream until thick. Transfer the tender chicken to a plate and top with the sauce from the pan. Makes one serving.

Bayou Whipped Potatoes

6 baking potatoes
24 red potatoes
1 tablespoon chopped garlic
½ cup horseradish
2 teaspoons white pepper
2 teaspoons Lawry's Season Salt
½ pound whole butter
2 cups heavy cream maximum, heated
Mozarella and Cheddar cheese blend

Wash potatoes but DO NOT peel. Cut into large cubes and cook in pot of water until soft but not mushy. Drain well. Put potatoes in mixer. Add garlic, horseradish, pepper and salt, and mix on medium speed until all lumps disappear and the mixture is smooth. Add butter in chunks and cream until the potatoes are fluffy. Serve in a ramekin, or small dish, and top with the cheese blend and briefly place under a broiler or in a microwave to melt the cheese.

La Palma Mexican Restaurant

Bellefontaine, OH

2201 South Main Street
Bellefontaine, OH 43311
(937) 592-1601 - Bellefontaine
(937) 652-4999 - Urbana
www.lapalmabarandgrill.com

This is certainly one of the most vibrantly multi-colored restaurants I have visited. There are brightly painted signs of all sizes everywhere listing the specials, the general menu items, upcoming events and more. The atmosphere is so stimulating and exciting that it caught me by surprise when I entered the place. In fact, it took me a minute to get used to it, but I really enjoyed the setting.

The food is authentic Mexican fare, i.e. Steak Mexicano, Fajita Quesadilla Texicana and a variety of combination meals. Located on the outskirts of Bellefontaine, La Palma is a welcome sight in an otherwise sea of fast food restaurants. It is a good place to get charged up for the ski slopes in the winter at Mad River Mountain conveniently located nearby or visit the local golf courses or horseback riding stables in the summer or fall. The central Ohio scenery is beautiful most any time of the year especially in the rolling hills.

Beef Chimichangas

Sometimes chimichangas are deep-fried, but they can also be baked with less mess. The filling can be used as a filling for burritos as well.

1 pound ground beef
¾ cup onion, chopped
3 tablespoons canned green chilis, diced
1 clove garlic, minced
¼ teaspoon oregano, ground
¼ teaspoon cumin, ground
2½ cups taco sauce
1 16-ounce can refried beans
8 12-inch tortillas
3 tablespoons butter, melted
16 ounces Jack or Monterey Jack cheese, shredded

Preheat oven to 400 degrees. Brown beef over a medium heat. Stir and break into small pieces while it cooks. Drain grease and add onion, chilies, and garlic, and cook until tender. Add oregano, cumin and taco sauce. Mix well and let simmer on low heat until all ingredients are blended and slightly bubbling. Warm beans in a separate pan. Brush both side of each tortilla with butter and then spread a spoonful of beans down the middle of each tortilla followed by a generous portion of the beef mixture. Top with cheese and close by rolling up each tortilla tightly being careful not to tear them. Fold each side to the center to fully enclose the filling. Place each one seam-side down in a 9 x 13 inch baking dish. Bake until golden brown. Additional cheese or salsa may be added when served. Chicken or shrimp can be substituted for the beef.

Burritos

An easy to make dish at home, burritos are warmed corn or wheat floured tortillas that are a hand-held food and a meal-in-one filled with healthy ingredients.

6 corn or wheat flour tortillas
1 tablespoon olive oil
1 onion, diced
1 16-ounce can refried beans
1 cup Monterey Jack cheese
2 14.5-ounce jars of salsa, your choice of mild to hot
1 cup sour cream
1 head lettuce, shredded
2 tomatoes, diced

The tortillas should be warmed so that they are tender and flexible. Preheat oven to 250 degrees. Then place each tortilla in a large lightly oiled pan on medium heat. Warm each side for 1 minute. Place each on a tray and cover with a warm dish towel and keep warm in the oven. Sauté onions in a medium pan and when transparent add the refried beans. Mix and warm thoroughly. While they are cooking place the cheese, salsa, sour cream, lettuce and tomatoes in separate bowls as well as the beans. Remove the warm tortillas from the oven and arrange on a plate and let your guests build their own burritos. Suggestion: start by putting refried beans down the middle of the tortilla followed by salsa, sour cream, lettuce, tomatoes, and cheese in that order.

CENTRAL WEST

Oscar's

Washington Court House, OH

A little bad news -good news here. The bad news is that Oscars is no longer in business as of this writing. However, the good news is that owners Jason Gilmore and Nathan Zukowitz have continued their catering business providing area organizations, private parties, and weddings with the same elegant service and fine cuisine they offered at their restaurant.

During my initial visit when I was writing the *Eating Your Way Across Ohio* book, Jason shared the following recipe with me that is just a small example of what they served in the restaurant, and what they no doubt offer on their catering menu.

I'm not sure whether they will make another go at the restaurant business. It certainly is difficult to say, but with their talent, at least they are still in the food service industry.

Pineapple Dressing

½ cup butter
3 cups sugar
6 eggs, lightly beaten
½ cup Half and Half
Pinch salt
6 slices bread, cubed
2 large cans, pineapple, crushed and drained
¼ cup cinnamon

Preheat oven to 350 degrees. Melt butter in a 9 x 11 inch baking dish and set aside. Mix together 2½ cups of sugar, beaten eggs, Half and Half, and salt until thoroughly blended. Gently add bread cubes and carefully fold in pineapple so as not to break up the bread cubes. Make sure that both the bread and pineapple are thoroughly coated.

Pour mixture into a baking dish and firmly press it in place in order to eliminate air pockets. Mix remaining sugar and cinnamon and sprinkle generously over the mixture. Bake for 45 minutes. Serve warm.

CENTRAL WEST

Peach's Grill

Yellow Springs, OH

104 Xenia Avenue
Yellow Springs, OH 45387
(937) 767-4850
www.peachsgrill.com

It is hard to describe Yellow Springs, home of the revived Antioch College, but I found it fun, quaint and quirky. Many artisans are located in this area so there are a number of small boutiques that offer one-of-a-kind handmade items and cater to those searching for unique gifts. The town and the shops are a great place to browse on a lovely sunny day and once you have found that prized piece of artwork or silver bracelet, then it is time for refreshment.

The motto at Peach's Grill says it all: "Simple Food for a Complex Community." Located on the edge of town, this converted drive-through has an open-air porch, and large twin dining rooms, each with its own beautifully crafted bar.

Peach's serves the usual bar food, like Spinach and Artichoke Dip with crispy homemade pita chips, BBQ Wings, and Cheesy Nachos. But they also offer specials like Sun-dried Tomato Feta and Chicken Salad with grapes, nuts and celery which is a tasty spin on an old time favorite. Most of their ingredients are fresh and complement their beverages, adult and otherwise.

Check their really cool web site for more information.

Spinach And Artichoke Dip

2 bags of spinach
1 can artichoke hearts
1 cup olive oil
2 pints heavy whipping cream
2/3 of an 8-ounce package of cream cheese
1 8-ounce container sour cream
6 tablespoons garlic salt
2 tablespoons oregano

2 tablespoons basil
1 large container of Parmesan cheese

In a large skillet, sauté spinach and artichoke hearts in olive oil until tender. In a large mixing bowl, combine whipping cream, cream cheese, sour cream, garlic salt, oregano and basil, and mix until all is thoroughly blended. Gently fold in the spinach, artichoke hearts and the Parmesan until the hearts are coated with the cream and cheese blend. Serve with chips.

The Purple Turtle Cafe

Washington Court House, OH

249 East Court Street
Washington Court House, OH 43160
(740) 636-0950
Check them out on Facebook

I'm not sure where the name Purple Turtle originated, but I do know that this little restaurant serves some of the healthiest food around. Brandon Long and his wife Tia initially opened the restaurant, but turned over ownership to his sister, Heather Walker, in 2012.

She maintains the same philosophy and focus on healthy and nutritious meals as Brandon had, and she makes most everything from scratch, including all pastry items. She also purchases fresh fruits and vegetables locally when in season. When I spoke to her, she stressed that she was developing more vegan and vegetarian meals, but she was balancing her menu with meat dishes as well.

Purple Turtle's specialty is freshly made Stromboli and Black Bean Tortillas, but their desserts explode with flavor especially the Black Raspberry Chocolate Scone. I had never eaten a scone before, but now I understand why the British stop everything for their afternoon tea and scones. I don't blame them. What an enjoyable custom to engage in while relaxing in this delightful atmosphere.

Chicken Enchilada Soup

6 ounces green chili peppers, chopped
1 small yellow or white onion
2 to 4 cloves of garlic, pressed
1 pound boneless, skinless chicken breast
Salt to taste
8 ounces cream cheese
4 cups chicken broth
1 cup all purpose flour
Fresh, finely shredded Cheddar cheese for garnish (optional)
Tortilla strips (optional)

Preheat oven to 350 degrees. In a roasting pan, spread green chili peppers, onion, and garlic over the chicken breasts. Lightly salt. Cover and bake until chicken is thoroughly cooked, about 20 to 30 minutes.

In a large saucepan, melt the cream cheese, stirring constantly to avoid scorching. Once melted, add broth and flour. Continue to stir with a whisk until it begins to thicken. Once the chicken reaches a minimum internal temperature of 165 degrees, allow it to cool slightly and then chop the meat coarsely. Add chopped chicken to the rest of the contents of the roasting pan in the soup base. Allow soup to simmer for about 10 minutes, stirring occasionally to avoid burning. Garnish with shredded Cheddar cheese and tortilla strips. Serves about 4.

Chocolate Mousse

3½ ounces chocolate with 70-85% cocoa
¼ cup sugar
3 egg yolks
1 cup heavy cream

Whipped Cream
2 tablespoons sugar
1 cup heavy cream

Melt chocolate in a double boiler until it is barely melted and set it aside. In a heavy sauce pan, combine sugar, egg yolks and heavy cream and stir constantly until it starts to bubble. Combine melted chocolate and cream mixture. Mix well. Cover and place in refrigerator to cool, at least 1 hour.

Once the chocolate mixture is cool, whip up an additional cup of heavy cream with the additional sugar to form stiff peaks. Fold the cooled chocolate mixture together with the whipped cream. Use as a stand alone dessert served in fancy (or not so fancy) dishes. Or use in a cake recipe or as a pie filling.

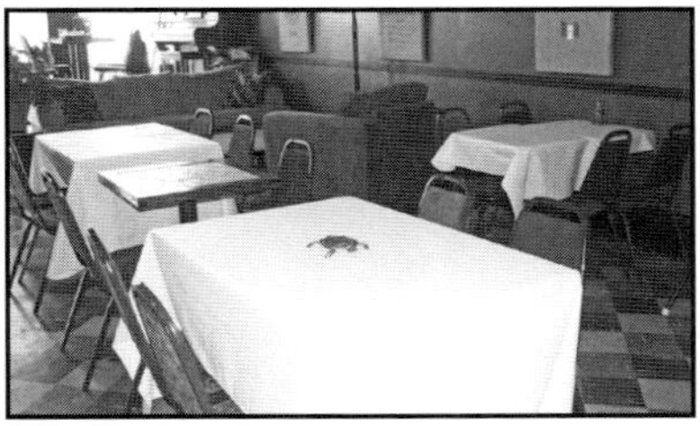

The Refectory

Columbus, OH

1092 Bethel Road
Columbus, OH 43220
(614) 451-9774
www.therefectoryrestaurant.com

I think everyone should have a special place where they celebrate the significant moments in their lives, and the Refectory has been the setting for a lifetime of memories for our family. From anniversaries and birthdays to engagement parties and rehearsal dinners, I consider this one of the best restaurants in central Ohio.

This elegant five-star restaurant is set in a rustic 1850s church that was converted in 1976 to what would eventually be the French restaurant of the 21st century in central Ohio. Born, raised and trained in Lyon, France, Chef Richard Blondin is the creative genius who develops the exquisite menu that we savor, whether we are celebrating or simply searching for a fabulous dining experience. I highly recommend this superb restaurant.

Pheasant Terrine

1 pheasant, skinned and carcass stripped of meat
16 ounces pork shoulder
8 ounces chicken liver
8 ounces veal shoulder
1 onion
3 tablespoons parsley, finely chopped
2 tablespoons brandy
2 whole eggs
Salt and black pepper
8 ounces smoked bacon
3 bay leaves

Once the meat is removed from the carcasses, grind the pheasant, pork, chicken liver, veal, and onion together. Add the parsley, brandy, whole eggs, salt and pepper and stir together very well. Line a lidded ovenproof dish with the bacon, but save a few strips to use on the top of the dish. Put all of the meat mixture into the bacon-lined dish, cover with the remaining bacon and place a bay leaf on top.

Cook in a bain marie* at 350 degrees for 1½ hours. Let cool overnight in the refrigerator, then slice and serve. Serves 14 guests.

(* A bain-marie is like a double boiler because it is a container that is used to heat food in other containers.)

Warm Apple Tart With Rosemary

10 ounces frozen puff pastry
Parchment
5 Golden Delicious apples (may substitute Anjou pears)
⅓ cup plus 4 tablespoons sugar
½ cup unsalted butter, divided in half
½ teaspoon fresh rosemary leaves, chopped fine
3 tablespoons sifted powdered sugar
4 unblemished mint sprigs

Thaw the pastry, and on a floured surface roll it out to ½ inch thickness. Cut out 4 rounds, each 5 inches in diameter. Transfer the rounds to a baking sheet lined with parchment and refrigerate for at least 25 minutes. Peel, core, and finely dice 1 apple (or pear). Place it in a small saucepan with a ½ cup of sugar and half the butter. Cook over low heat until the fruit is very soft and the sugar is dissolved to make a spreadable compote. Set the pan aside to cool.

Preheat the oven to 350 degrees. Cut four 6 inch squares of parchment. Arrange the squares on a baking sheet and sprinkle 2 tablespoons of sugar evenly over the sheets. Place the pastry rounds on top of the sugar and prick the entire surface of the dough with a fork. Spread a tablespoon of cooled fruit compote over each pastry round. Sprinkle the rosemary evenly over the compote.

Peel, core and thinly slice the remaining apples (or pears). Fan the slices out in a circular pattern on top of the tarts. In a small saucepan, melt the remaining butter. With a pastry brush, coat the tops of the tarts carefully. Sprinkle the remaining 2 tablespoons of sugar over the tarts. Bake for 18 minutes, or until the apples begin to caramelize, turning light golden brown.

Serve hot on dessert plates, dusted with powdered sugar and garnish with a mint sprig. Makes 4 individual servings.

CENTRAL WEST

Tuscan Table

Circleville, OH

122 North Court Street
Circleville, OH 43113
(740) 477-3040
www.the-tuscantable.com

If you enjoy Italian cuisine, Tuscan Table is the real thing. Located in downtown Circleville, its motto says it all – *"A Casual Family Friendly Italian Restaurant."* The atmosphere is casual, but the cuisine is authentic Italian with Manicotti, Eggplant Parmesan, Blackened Chicken Fettuccini, Shrimp Pomodoro, and Italian Spaghetti and Meatballs topped with the chef's homemade sauce. The Chicken Milanese, which means "chicken in the style of Milan," is excellent, especially with the creamy housemade Alfredo sauce. Portions are generous and will surely fill the void for most any guest, often with plenty to take home.

As the motto indicates, this is a family friendly place that accommodates a variety of tastes. With that in mind, the Build Your Own Pizza is very popular with kids, teens, and even adults. This feature is designed to let the guest choose from a selection of sauces, cheese, meats and veggies according to his or her own preferences. It is fun to watch the pizzas and, for that matter, all the dishes being prepared from your table with the kitchen clearly in view. As each dish is completed, it is ready to be delivered to a hungry diner.

When you are in town for the Pumpkin Show in October and want something more than fair food, drop by Tuscan Table for a fine meal and a great dining experience.

Minnestrone

2 cups onions, diced
1 tablespoon garlic
2 cups celery, chopped
½ cup olive oil or a blend
5 quarts water
½ container chicken base
1 pound zucchini

1 pound yellow squash
1 pound carrots, chopped
1 large can of diced tomatoes
3 tablespoons parsley
1/8 cup pesto
1 cup white wine
1 tablespoon salt
1 tablespoon pepper
1 cup ditalini pasta, cooked

Sauté onions, garlic and celery in oil on low heat until vegetables are tender. Dissolve the chicken base in warm water. Add zucchini, squash, carrots and tomatoes and stir. Season with parsley, pesto, wine, salt and pepper and bring soup to a boil. Turn down the heat and simmer for 10 minutes. Add the pasta and cook until just tender. Serve in tureens with Italian bread, if desired.

Alfredo Sauce

2 pounds butter
1 8-ounce cream cheese
6 quarts heavy cream
2 tablespoons kosher salt
3 tablespoons cracked black pepper
3 tablespoons garlic
4½ cups Parmesan cheese
4½ cups Romano cheese

Melt the butter in a large pan on medium to low heat being careful not to burn the butter. Slowly add the cream cheese and whisk constantly. Over a medium heat, stir the heavy cream into the butter and cheese mixture making sure that the ingredients are thoroughly blended. Season with salt, pepper, and garlic and slowly fold in the Parmesan and Romano cheeses. Continue to adjust the heat and stir frequently to prevent scalding and to assure that all ingredients are mixed well. Taste and adjust the flavor if necessary. Serve on your choice of pasta.

Werner's Smokehouse

Jeffersonville, OH

11396 Allen Road
Jeffersonville, OH 43128
(740) 948-2989
www.wernersbbq.com

A tasty way of finishing up a day of shopping at the Jeffersonville outlet stores is to cross the street to Werner's, located on the corner of State Route 35 and Interstate 71. Not only does barbecue take on a life of its own here in most every entrée, but the side dishes reminded me of family picnics when I was growing up. I always thought my grandmother made the best potato salad, but Werner's comes in as a very close second.

To balance the spicy BBQ taste, there are a number of delicious desserts to choose from including Key Lime Pie, which is only one of many recipes handed down to Marsha Arnold, the owners' daughter and restaurant manager. Not only does she manage the restaurant, Marsha also oversees the catering business that provides full meals to tired travelers at local motels.

Potato Salad

This potato salad is served at all of Marsha's family gatherings, but it is a popular item in the restaurant and the catering menu as well.

5 pounds red potatoes
6 eggs
1½ cups sugar
3 tablespoons flour
¾ teaspoon salt
¾ cup red wine vinegar
¾ cup water
1½ tablespoons mustard
2½ cups mayonnaise
1 onion, finely diced
Celery, finely diced

Thoroughly scrub and cut red potatoes into small bite size pieces, place in a saucepan of water and cook until tender. Drain the water and place potatoes in a large bowl and set aside. Combine the eggs, sugar, flour, salt, vinegar, water and mustard together and place in another pan. Slowly bring the mixture to a boil and cook until thickened. Stir in mayonnaise and continue to cook until warm and well blended. Pour the dressing mixture over the potatoes and gently mix until potatoes are covered. Top with the onion and celery which combines nicely with the color of the potatoes. Cool and serve.

Key Lime Pie

3 ounces of cream cheese, softened
½ cup lime juice
14 ounces sweetened condensed milk
6 ounces whipped topping
2 drops green food coloring
1 graham cracker crust

Combine the cream cheese and lime juice together with a mixer. Slowly add the sweetened condensed milk and mix thoroughly to achieve a smooth lump-free texture. Add the whipped topping and food coloring making sure to blend well and distribute the food coloring evenly throughout the cheese mixture. Pour into a pie shell and refrigerate in order to let the filling set up and become firm. Garnish with key lime slices.

Fresh Peach Pie

5 to 6 peaches, peeled and sliced
Fruit Fresh

<u>Glaze</u>
1 cup sugar
3 tablespoons cornstarch
1 cup water
1 3.5-ounce box peach Jell-O
1 teaspoon almond extract
2 drops yellow food coloring

1 baked 9-inch pie crust
Cool Whip

Peel peaches, drain if juicy, and sprinkle with Fruit Fresh. In a separate pan, bring the sugar, cornstarch, and water to a boil and cook until thick and bubbly, stirring constantly to avoid sticking or burning. Remove from heat and add 3 tablespoons of peach Jell-O, almond extract and food coloring. Mix thoroughly. Allow to cool to room temperature. Carefully fold peaches into cooled glaze and pour the mixture into baked crust. Refrigerate until set. Top with Cool Whip.

Young's Jersey Dairy

Yellow Springs, OH

6880 Springfield Xenia Road
Yellow Springs, OH 45387
(937) 325-0629
www.youngsdairy.com

Young's is one of the oldest businesses in Green County with a history dating back to 1869. My visit quickly reminded me of times when life was simpler and food came directly from the farm. Being a country girl, I love the smell of fresh flowers, the sight of abundant gardens and the sound of roosters crowing in the barnyard. Young's has it all especially baby goats, which I'm particularly partial to, and a herd of cows that provide the main ingredient in their homemade ice cream.

This is a charming place that provides the whole family with a real country experience from touring the grounds and buildings, visiting the animals, and finishing up with a down home meal at the restaurant or a sweet snack at the dairy store.

Sweet Potato Casserole

5 pounds sweet potatoes, peeled and cut in 1-inch chunks
1 cup granulated sugar
½ cup butter, melted
2 eggs
1 teaspoon vanilla
½ cup milk

Topping:
1 cup light brown sugar
½ cup flour
⅓ cup butter, melted
1 cup pecan pieces

In a large pot, boil the potato chunks until tender. Cool and add to the granulated sugar, butter, eggs, vanilla and milk. Mix well until it makes a smooth paste. Pour into a greased 9 x 13 inch pan. In a separate bowl, blend the brown sugar, flour, butter and pecan pieces together and sprinkle over the sweet potato mixture. Bake at 375 degrees for 35 to 45 minutes or until the top is slightly brown. Cool 15 minutes before serving.

Bread Pudding with Cinnamon Sugar Topping

<u>Cinnamon Topping</u>:

¼ cup granulated sugar
1⅓ teaspoons cinnamon

7 eggs
1 cup granulated sugar
3½ cups milk
3½ cups cream
1 tablespoon vanilla extract
1 teaspoon nutmeg
⅓ teaspoon salt
¾ loaf white bread, cut into 1½ inch squares

Preheat oven to 375 degrees. Mix the cinnamon and sugar together and set aside. Whisk eggs and sugar in a large bowl to blend well. And whisk the milk, cream, vanilla, nutmeg, and salt into the egg mixture. Fold in bread pieces and let stand for 5 minutes. Pour the mixture into a 9 x 13 inch greased pan and top with the sugar and cinnamon topping. Bake uncovered for 45 to 55 minutes until golden brown on top and slightly loose in the middle when shaken. The internal temperature should be 165 degrees. Let cool slightly. Serve with a caramel sauce or Young's French Vanilla ice cream for a real treat. Store covered in the refrigerator.

Honey BBQ Chicken

There are two ways to make Honey BBQ Chicken. Take your pick: either grilled or baked. Both ways will yield a tender and sweet/spicy meat.

1 whole chicken, cut into pieces
2 cups ketchup
2 cups granulated sugar
4 tablespoons honey

Thoroughly mix ketchup, sugar and honey together and set aside.

Grill the chicken over medium heat until almost done, about 35 to 45 minutes. Frequently baste the chicken with the sauce, turning the pieces often so that the sauce does not burn.

Bake the chicken by laying the pieces out without overlapping in a large pan or two smaller pans. Coat the meat with the sauce by brushing or pouring it over the chicken. Bake at 350 degrees for 35 to 45 minutes. Baste with the sauce while baking. If the chicken browns too quickly, cover it with foil.

CENTRAL EAST
REGION

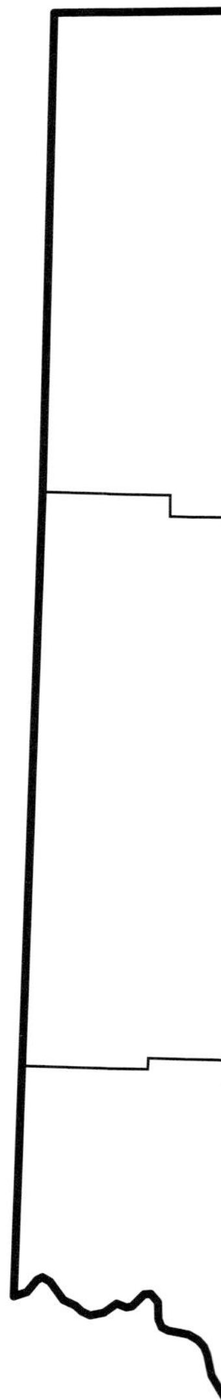

Boondock's BBQ & Grill	McConnelsville, OH
Buxton Inn	Granville, OH
Clay Haus	Somerset, OH
The Forum	Cambridge, OH
The Granville Inn	Granville, OH
Main Street Grill & Café	St. Clairsville, OH
Nutcracker Family Restaurant	Pataskala, OH
Roots	Lancaster, OH
Shaw's	Lancaster, OH
Short Story Brassiere	Granville, OH
Tom's Ice Cream Bowl	Zanesville, OH
Warehouse Steak n' Stein	Coshocton, OH

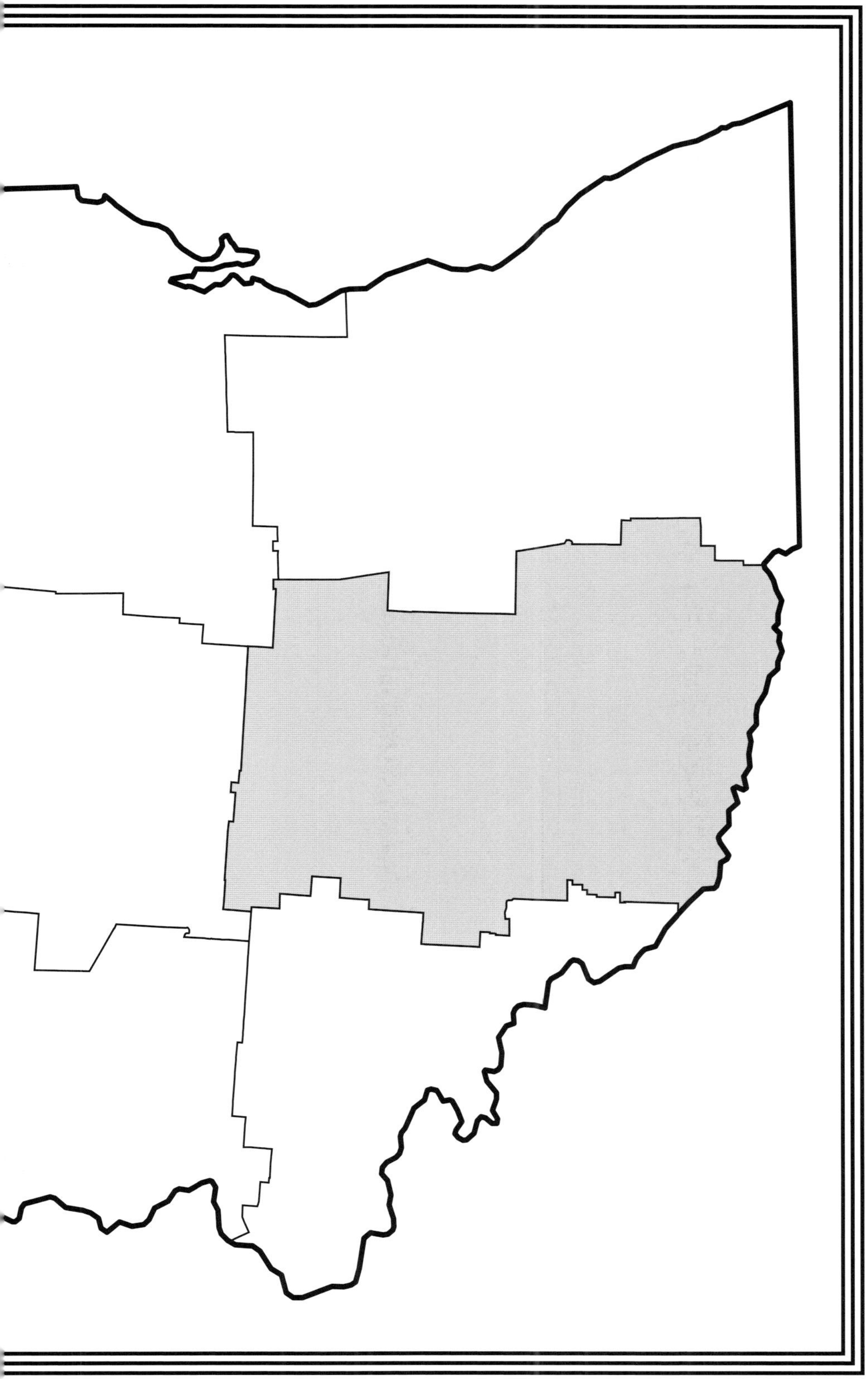

Boondock's BBQ & Grill

McConnelsville, OH

4653 North State Route 60
McConnelsville, OH 43756
(740) 962-4100
Check them ot on Facebook

Boondock's, located in McConnelsville on the bank of the Muskingum River, is one of the few places in Ohio to be featured on the television show "Diners, Drive-ins and Dives" which is quite an honor.

Owners Bobby "BJ" Murdette and his wife Maria shared with me their burning desire to own and manage their own restaurant. Both are educated and experienced chefs and they have created an extensive menu based on their education and knowledge of their market especially their customers' culinary preferences.

Though there are many choices on the menu, the ribs take top billing and BJ's customized rub and cooking style is what tenderizes the meat so that it falls literally off the bone. I felt fortunate that he wanted to share this recipe with my readers. This is like finding gold. The Crab Cake recipe was just an added bonus. Enjoy!

Rib Rub

2 cups brown sugar
½ cup chili powder
⅓ cup Liquid Smoke
2 tablespoons kosher salt
½ tablespoon ground black pepper
2 tablespoons paprika
2 tablespoons granulated garlic
1 teaspoon onion powder
½ teaspoon cayenne pepper powder

Whisk all ingredients together in a bowl and apply the rub evenly on raw ribs that have been patted dry. For the best results, let the rubbed meat sit for at least 6 hours before cooking. This rub is easy to make and provides a good balance of saltiness and sweetness that brings out the flavor of the meat. The remaining unused rub can be refrigerated in an airtight container.

Louisiana Crab Cakes

1 pound crab meat, shredded
1½ tablespoons dry bread crumbs
2 teaspoons chopped fresh parsley
Salt and pepper to taste
1 egg
1 tablespoon Cajun seasoning
1½ tablespoons mayonnaise
½ teaspoon ground dry mustard
1 dash hot pepper sauce

Preheat oven broiler. In a large bowl mix together crab meat, bread crumbs, parsley, salt and pepper. Set aside. In a small bowl, beat egg and add Cajun seasoning, mayonnaise, mustard and pepper sauce. Combine with the other ingredients in the large bowl and mix together thoroughly. Form into palm-sized patties and place on a lightly greased broiler pan or baking sheet about ½ to ¾ inches apart. Broil for 10 to 15 minutes until lightly brown. Serve with tartar or other preferred sauce.

Buxton Inn

Granville, OH

313 East Broadway Street
Granville, OH 43023
(740) 587-0001
www.buxtoninn.com

What can I say about an establishment that was founded in 1812 and is still in business today? As a former way station at the crossroads of the old stagecoach run serving central Ohio, the Buxton Inn provided shelter and food to travelers year round.

The beautifully restored and maintained building has remarkably passed the test of time thanks to its caring owner, Robert Schilling. This rambling building has so many nooks and crannies, rooms and hallways that it's like a maze. There are seven dining areas to choose from, plus a spacious patio surrounded by former flower gardens and a sizeable water fountain. How relaxing!

Rumors have circulated for years that friendly ghosts reside in these walls. I wouldn't be surprised considering the number of people who have stayed under Buxton's roof over the decades. But there is nothing that should deter you from feeling comfortable enough to stay overnight or at least dropping by for lunch or dinner. It is truly an experience to absorb the ambiance of yesteryear.

Sweet Cream Chicken Salad

1 chicken breast, finely diced
½ cup red or green grapes, chopped
⅓ cup toasted walnuts, chopped
½ cup celery, finely diced
Celery salt, pinch

Sweet Cream Dressing:

¼ cup sugar
1 cup mayonnaise
1 tablespoon vinegar
1 teaspoon mustard, not dry
1 tablespoon cream
Celery salt

In a medium sized bowl, mix the chicken breast, grape pieces, walnuts and celery. In a separate bowl, make the Sweet Cream Dressing by combining the sugar, mayonnaise, vinegar, mustard and cream. Mix the dressing with the chicken salad and add a pinch of celery salt. This dressing can also be used in potato salad and macaroni salad.

Gazpacho

As a dedicated all year around soup lover, I prefer mine hot, BUT this blender free gazpacho recipe is delicious especially for lunch on a hot summer day. And it is brimming with nutritious ingredients.

¼ cup green peppers, diced
¼ sweet red peppers, diced
½ cup celery, diced
½ cup scallions with tops, diced
½ cup cucumbers, seeded, soaked in iced salt water and diced
¼ clove garlic very finely minced
¼ cup parsley, minced
¼ cup fresh basil, minced
4 tomatoes, peeled, seeded and chopped

1 cup extra virgin olive oil
1 cup tomato juice
¼ cup vinegar
¼ teaspoon (or more) course black pepper
Salt and pepper to taste.

NO BLENDERS!! Finely dice the vegetables to the size of a kitchen match head. Combine the oil, tomato juice and vinegar in a stainless steel bowl, or earthen crock that is set down in a bowl of ice to chill. Stir in the vegetables and herbs, then add the salt and pepper. Serve as cold as possible with hot buttered toast.

Clay Haus

Somerset, OH

123 West Main Street
Somerset, OH 43783
(740) 743-1326
www.clayhaus.com

The Clay Haus was built between 1812 and 1820 and it has been beautifully maintained in the style of that era. Obvious updates have been necessary, like indoor plumbing, electricity and a fully functional kitchen. It has served as a restaurant for years, owned by the Snider family since 1979, and is currently owned and managed by Scott Snider who took over after his parents passed away.

Scott has been dedicated to preserving the German influence not only in the décor and furnishings, but also in the menu. The following recipes are only two examples.

German Potato Salad

6 large potatoes, peeled and boiled
½ pound of bacon, 8 to 10 slices
½ cup onions, diced
1 cup vinegar
2 cups water
1 cup brown sugar
1 tablespoon salt
1 teaspoon pepper
Flour or cornstarch

Slice cooled potatoes into mixing bowl and set aside. Brown the bacon and onion together in a large skillet until fat is gone from the bacon then add vinegar and water. Bring this mixture to a boil stirring in the brown sugar, salt and pepper. Adjust the salt and pepper to taste. Thicken this mixture by gradually adding flour or cornstarch.

When a consistency of smooth, lump free sauce is achieved, gently stir the mixture into the sliced potatoes. Serve warm.

Sauerbraten

3 to 4 pounds chuck roast
Salt and pepper
½ cup pearl onions
¾ cup celery, chunked
¾ cup mini carrots
½ cup vinegar
1 cup red wine
1 cup water
1 tablespoon salt
1 tablespoon peppercorns
½ tablespoon allspice
1 bay leaf
½ to 1 cup sour cream, as desired
1 cup ginger snaps

Preheat oven to 350 degrees. Place chuck roast in roasting pan, and salt and pepper the meat. Add the remaining ingredients in roasting pan except sour cream and ginger snaps. Layer the top of the roast with ginger snaps and pour a little of the liquid around the roast over the snaps. Cover and bake 2 to 3 hours until tender.

Remove roast and vegetables from the liquid and stir in sour cream. Thicken to desired consistency. Slice roast and serve with the vegetables. Lace with sour cream gravy. Serves 4 to 6.

The Forum

Cambridge, OH

2205 Southgate Parkway
Cambridge, OH 43725
(740) 439-2777
www.theforumrestaurant.com

The Forum is easy to find because it is located right off I-70 at the Cambridge exit on Southgate Parkway. This elegant pristine restaurant owned by Alex and Karen Theodosopoulos offers a complete menu of authentic Greek cuisine the likes of which can be found in the Greek Isles.

The following selections reflect the owners' heritage and are family recipes passed down through generations. They are just a sampling of what to expect when you visit The Forum.

Pizza Soup

2½ quarts of water
8 ounces green peppers, diced
8 ounces mushrooms, sliced
8 ounces white onions, diced
24 ounces pizza sauce
24 ounces tomatoes, crushed
28 ounces tomatoes, diced plus juice
12 ounces pepperoni, slices
12 ounces Italian sausage, cooked in small chunks
2 tablespoons fresh garlic, chopped
2 tablespoons Italian seasoning
2 tablespoons oregano
Mozzarella cheese

Heat the water but do not boil. Add all the ingredients to the water. Make sure the sausage is in small bite size chunks. Stir to mix well. Simmer for 15 to 20 minutes until vegetables are slightly tender, but not overcooked. Serve with grated Mozzarella cheese.

Soulaki Over Rice

1 to 2 pound pork tenderloin
Pita bread
White rice, cooked
Lettuce
Tomato
Creamy Tzatzkiki sauce, optional

Marinade
4 ounces olive oil
4 ounces lemon juice
1 tablespoon red wine vinegar
1 tablespoon garlic, minced
1 tablespoon oregano, dried or fresh
3 ounces onion, finely chopped
1 tablespoon seasoning salt

Cut pork into 1-inch pieces and place in a glass bowl. Pour marinade over the meat, cover and refrigerate for 24 hours. Take out of the refrigerator and drain marinade. You may reserve the marinade to add to the steamed rice if desired for added flavor. Put the pieces of pork on wooden skewers, 6 to 10 pieces per serving, and charbroil until cooked thoroughly. Remove meat from skewers and place on grilled pita bread. Serve with creamy Greek Tzatzkiki sauce and a scoop of rice.

Parisian Sauce

2 quarts of heavy whipping cream, heated but not boiling
1½ pounds of Cheddar and Monterey Jack cheeses, shredded
5 ounces Swiss cheese, sliced
4 ounces Grey Poupon country mustard
4 ounces Parmesan cheese, grated
2 ounces Chablis wine
3 ounces Cajun seasoning

Roux:
12 tablespoons (1½ sticks) melted butter
12 ounces all purpose flour

Combine all ingredients in a food processor, except for the heated whipping cream, in order to mix them together but not pulverize them. Set aside.

Make a roux to thicken the mixture by melting the butter in a pan on medium heat and gradually whisk in the flour until it is a slightly thick consistency. Turn heat to low and cover. Mix the ingredients from the food processor with the heated cream and stir until all is melted. When this is achieved, gradually add the roux to thicken the cream mixture being careful to stir constantly to avoid sticking or the formation of lumps. The right consistency should be a little thicker than gravy. Use this sauce over Parisian Seafood with fettuccini.

CENTRAL EAST

Granville Inn

Granville, OH

314 East Broadway Street
Granville, OH 43023
(888) 472-6855

The Granville Inn is a beautiful Jacobethan Revival style structure located on the edge of this charming village and houses spacious dining areas, a banquet facility and a modernized hotel with 27 rooms and three suites. Its fascinating history stretches back to 1927 when the mansion was constructed on the location of the former Granville Female College.

Over the years, ownership has changed hands as the Inn fell on hard times. Most recently, Denison University, located nearby, purchased it and has agreed to keep it open and operating in the same manner as it has for decades. This is good news because these two institutions represent a wealth of Granville history.

One of the Inn's signature dishes is the chicken salad which is touted to be the same recipe as the popular dish served in the Chintz Room of the now defunct Lazarus Department Store located in downtown Columbus.

After some research, I was able to find the Lazarus recipe which is a true classic. Enjoy!

Lazarus Chicken Salad

2 cups cubed chicken
1½ cups celery, diced
¼ cup onion, diced
2 tablespoons pecans, chopped
1 tablespoon lemon juice
1 teaspoon salt
¼ teaspoon pepper
1 tablespoon Worcestershire sauce
1 cup Miracle Whip
Croissants

Mix the chicken, celery, onion, pecans and lemon juice together. Season with salt, pepper, and adjust seasoning to taste. Add Worcestershire sauce. Mix thoroughly and fold in Miracle Whip. Serve on small croissants with a side of fresh fruit.

CENTRAL EAST

Main Street Grill & Café

St. Clairsville, OH

St. Clairsville, OH
110 West Main Street St.
Clairsville, OH 43950
(740) 296-5276

As the name implies, this eatery is located on Main Street in St. Clairsville on the other side of Interstate 70 not too far from the Ohio Valley Mall. It reflects a sophistication and elegance that one does not frequently find in a town this size. It is a very comfortable cozy café in the classic sense.

There is a brisk lunch crowd from local businesses especially from the Belmont County Court House across the street, as well as workers in the area.

Main Street Crab Cakes

3 eggs
¾ cup mayonnaise
1 tablespoon Old Bay seasoning
¾ tablespoon Cajun seasoning
1 tablespoon Monterey Chicken Seasoning
½ tablespoon thyme
¼ cup white onion, diced
⅓ cup red pepper, diced
16 ounces lump crab meat
16 ounces crab claw meat
1 cup Panko bread crumbs
Butter

In a medium sized bowl, blend eggs and mayonnaise together with a spatula until smooth. Add seasoning, thyme, onions, and pepper, and mix well. Fold in crab and bread crumbs. Cover and refrigerate at least 30 minutes before portioning and shaping into 4-ounce patties. Pan fry both sides in little butter until golden brown.

Main Street Chili

5 pounds ground beef
1 cup chili powder divided into thirds
3 tablespoons beef base
3 tablespoons garlic
1 medium white onion, diced
3 bell peppers, diced
52-ounce can kidney beans
3 tablespoons Red Hot sauce
¼ cup honey
1/3 cup bourbon
32 ounces beer
48 ounces tomato juice
1 tablespoon salt
1 tablespoon pepper

Brown meat with 1/3 cup chili powder and beef base. Add garlic, onion, peppers, beans, second 1/3 cup chili powder, Red Hot, honey, and bourbon. Cook until soft. Deglaze or thin the mixture with beer and bring to a boil for 10 minutes. Reduce heat to simmer and add tomato juice and last 1/3 cup of chili powder. Add salt and pepper to taste. Simmer 30 minutes and remove from heat and cool.

Nutcracker Family Restaurant

Pataskala, OH

63 East Broad Street
Pataskala, OH 43062
(740) 964-0056
www.nutcrackerpataskala.com

This charming 1950s style restaurant has been a part of the Pataskala scene since it was an ice cream parlor located in downtown back in the 1950s. Nancy and Steve Butcher purchased the place in 1995 and subsequently moved to its current location on Broad Street. However, 10 years later a devastating fire destroyed the building and the Butchers embarked on the daunting task of rebuilding from the ground up. They chose to expand on the 1950s theme and while they were considering the items to include in the new restaurant, they amassed from friends and well wishers hundreds of nutcrackers that are prominently displayed throughout the place. They also added scores of authentic memorabilia from the era that brings back fond memories for anyone who lived during that time.

Steven and Nancy have generously shared the following recipes that give visitors an idea of what to expect to find on the menu at the Nutcracker. Quantities may have to be adjusted considering the number of servings desired.

Nutcracker Crab Cakes

1 pound flaked crab
¼ cup red bell peppers, finely diced
½ tablespoon dried cilantro
1 tablespoon fresh parsley, finely chopped
1 cup mayonnaise
3 eggs
1 cup corn flakes, crushed
1 tablespoon Dijon mustard
½ teaspoon Cayenne pepper
½ teaspoon Tabasco
¼ teaspoon garlic powder
¼ teaspoon onion powder

Combine all ingredients in a bowl and mix thoroughly. Form palm-sized patties and fry in a lightly buttered pan or on a foil lined grill to prevent crumbling through the cooking grate. Turn over when half way through the cooking process so that each side is golden brown. Serve with a side of dill sauce.

Dill Sauce
1 cup sour cream
2 tablespoons lemon juice
3 tablespoons Dijon mustard
4 teaspoons fresh dill, chopped

Combine all ingredients thoroughly. Place in covered bowl and chill before serving.

Corned Beef Hash

2½ pounds corned beef, shredded and finely chopped
3 pounds potatoes, shredded
1½ pounds onions, sautéed and finely chopped
1 tablespoon black pepper
1 bunch parsley, finely chopped
Butter
1 dozen eggs (optional)

Mix all ingredients together and cook in a lightly buttered pan or grill until golden brown. As an option, scramble a dozen eggs and add to the hash. For the best results, refrigerated overnight after mixing ingredients and before cooking. Each serving size is approximately 1 cup.

Ham Loaf

If you are feeding a group or want to make plan ahead meals to freeze, this is a favorite Nutcracker recipe.

1½ pounds ground ham
¾ pound ground pork
3 eggs
½ cup milk
⅓ cup tomato juice
1 cup bread crumbs
Salt and pepper

Preheat oven at 350 degrees. Thoroughly mix the ham, pork and eggs. Gradually add the milk and tomato juice to create a very moist meat mixture. Combine the bread crumbs to absorb some of the moisture resulting in a firm and malleable ball. Form 6 8-ounce loaves. Place in loaf pans and bake for 1 to 1 ½ hours. Glaze (see recipe below) the loaves during the last 15-20 minutes of cooking.

Ham Loaf Glaze
2 pounds brown sugar
1 teaspoon dry mustard
½ cup honey
1 cup apple juice
1½ cups vinegar
2 cups water
3 tablespoons cornstarch

Combine all ingredients in a large saucepan over medium heat. Stir well until mixture thickens and remove from heat. Spread evenly over each of the ham loaves.

NUTCRACKER
Family Restaurant

TIME TO EAT
Phone Ahead
Carryout

Roots

Lancaster, OH

1260 North Memorial Drive
Lancaster, OH 43130
(740) 653-8944
Check them out on Facebook

Roots is one of the few locally owned restaurants in Lancaster where you can get a "made from scratch" homemade meal, like Char-broiled Chicken and New York Strip Steak, or mouth watering desserts like Dutch Apple and Coconut Cream Pies. Located on Memorial Drive, the restaurant has occupied the original house of the former owners for more than 50 years, though it has been updated.

Thomas Wolfe said, "You can't go home again," but the warm and friendly atmosphere at Roots is about as close as you can get to being home. If you are a regular, everyone knows your name, like the Cheers of Lancaster, and other guests even ask about your day. Owner Janet Graff and her son, manager Chris Strawn, are gracious hosts. They always add a personal touch to the meal and are willing to go the extra mile to make a visit enjoyable.

Chris's Jumbalaya

1½ pounds ground Italian sausage
4 teaspoons oil
6 teaspoons garlic, chopped
4 cups onions, chopped
3 cups green peppers, chopped
1 cup parsley, chopped
6 cups canned diced tomatoes
4 bay leaves
1 teaspoon thyme, ground
½ teaspoon Cayenne pepper
5 cups rice, uncooked
8 cups water
3 pounds cooked meat (chicken, shrimp or link sausage)

Sauté sausage in oil for 3 minutes until brown. Add garlic, onion, green pepper, and cook over a medium heat until almost tender. Stir in parsley, tomatoes, bay leaves, thyme, and Cayenne pepper, and then add rice. Slowly stir in water and mix well. Add second meat: either chunked pieces of chicken or whole small or medium shrimp (remove tails) or sliced link sausage. Bring the mixture to a boil, stir well, cover and reduce heat to low. Simmer without stirring for 25 to 30 minutes until the liquid has been absorbed. Remove bay leaf before serving. Serves 10 to 12.

Prune Cake

6 eggs
2 cups oil
1½ cups brown sugar, firmly packed
1½ cups white sugar
2 teaspoons baking powder
2 teaspoons baking soda
2 teaspoons salt
2 teaspoons cinnamon
4 cups cake flour
2 teaspoons vanilla
2 cups whole prunes, boiled and drained

Preheat oven to 350 degrees. Beat eggs in a large bowl. Add oil and both the brown and white sugar. Mix well and set aside. Sift together in a small bowl the dry ingredients: baking powder, baking soda, salt, cinnamon and flour, and add to the egg mixture. Then add the vanilla and the prunes. Mix thoroughly. Divide evenly and pour into two greased 9 x 13 inch glass pans. Bake for 40 minutes. Let the cakes cool and then cut into serving size pieces. Glaze as described below.

Glaze:

⅓ pound butter
2 cups granulated sugar
1 cup buttermilk
1 teaspoon baking soda

Combine the butter, sugar, buttermilk and baking soda in a pan (not a double boiler) over medium heat and bring the mixture to a boil for 5 minutes. Pour over cut pieces of the cake and either serve warm or cold with warm glaze.

Shaw's

Lancaster, OH

123 North Broad Street
Lancaster, OH 43130
(800) 654-2477
www.shawsinn.com

Shaw's mission is to provide an elegant dining experience. Located in one of Lancaster's downtown historical buildings, the combination of exquisite atmosphere and exceptional cuisine fulfills their mission and creates a lasting memory; one that I first experienced decades ago when I lived in the area.

Shaw's menu selections, which change quarterly, range from casual to extraordinary and are designed with something for everyone. Check out their web site not only to find out their daily specials, but also their current events. Manager Susie Cork keeps busy with cooking classes and other events related to the restaurant especially during the popular Lancaster Festival in July.

Lobster Gazpacho

2½ pounds ripe tomatoes, chunked
2 bell peppers, any color
2 small yellow onions
3 green onions
2 cucumbers, peeled and seeded
4 large garlic cloves
2 tablespoons horseradish
¼ cup fresh cilantro
¼ cup fresh parsley
2 cups V-8 juice
2 cups tomato juice
2 tablespoons Worcestershire sauce
Juice of 2 lemons, about ¼ cup
Pinch of Cayenne pepper
Tabasco to taste

Puree all the above ingredients in a food processor in batches. Garnish with the following and chill until ready to serve.

Garnish:
2 pounds of cooked lobster meat, diced 1 inch pieces
1 cucumber, peeled, seeded, diced ¼ inch
1 bell pepper, any color, diced ¼ inch
3 green onions, sliced

Combine the ingredients in a medium bowl and gently mix well. Chill until ready to serve with the Lobster Gazpacho.

Almond Crusted Walleye with Blueberry Lime Butter

2 Walleye fillets
Salt and pepper
Vegetable oil
1 cup bread crumbs
1 cup toasted almonds
2 tablespoons fresh parsley

Season the fish with salt and pepper. Lightly coat with a bit of oil. In a shallow pan combine the crumbs, almonds and parsley. Dip the fish in the crumbs and set aside. Heat a saucepan on medium heat. Add about 2 tablespoons vegetable oil. Add the fish fillets and brown both sides. Top with the blueberry lime butter.

Blueberry Lime Butter:
1 stick butter, room temperature
1 lime zested* and juiced
Salt and pepper
½ cup fresh or frozen blueberries

Beat the butter in a mixer with a paddle until it is fluffy. Combine the lime zest* and squeeze the lime to extract the juice. Add to the butter. Season with salt and pepper. Add the blueberries and mix thoroughly. Taste and add more lime juice if needed.

(* Since the peel of a citrus fruit (lime, orange or lemon) provides valuable oil and flavor to a dish, the fruit can be "zested". This is done by washing and drying the fruit and slicing or scraping the peel carefully away from the flesh without cutting the pith (the white part). The peel is then finely cut up to form the consistency of confetti.) (www.coolthink.com)

Shaw's Crème Brulee

4 cups of heavy cream
½ vanilla bean, slit and scraped
Pinch of salt
10 egg yolks
5 tablespoons sugar
1 teaspoon real vanilla extract
1 to 2 teaspoons sugar

Preheat oven to 325 degrees. Heat cream with vanilla bean and salt in a medium saucepan until it comes to a boil. Whisk the yolks, sugar and vanilla extract in a bowl. Whisk in the hot cream. Mix well and strain. Ladle the custard into the dishes and place on a flat cookie sheet. Place the sheet in the oven and pour hot water around the ramekins until it comes about 1/3 of the way up the sides. Be careful not to get water in the custard. Bake about 35 to 50 minutes or until the center is set. Chill until ready to serve. Right before serving sprinkle each Brulee with about 1 to 2 tablespoons of sugar and carefully burn the top with a torch to caramelize the sugar.

Short Story Brassiere

Granville, OH

For reasons unknown to this writer, James Housteau, owner of the Short Story Brassiere, has closed his restaurant as well as his well known wine shop, the Wine Cache. As a world traveler, Mr. Housteau developed a taste for international cuisine which he featured in his elegant bistro along with a collection of fine wines. It is a loss to the Granville community, but I hope that he will take his exquisite talent for pairing food and wine and apply it to another worthwhile venture.

Fortunately, Mr. Housteau shared a few recipes with me when I visited with him months before he closed that provided a sampling of the culinary creations designed by he and his executive chef.

Pan Roasted Crab Cakes with Saffron Mustard Aioli

1 can high quality lump crab meat
¼ cup chives, chopped
2 tablespoons dill, chopped
¼ cup mayonnaise
2 tablespoons Dijon mustard
2 teaspoons Old Bay seasoning
1 egg, beaten

¼ cup bread crumbs
Extra bread crumbs for breading
Olive oil

Combine the first 7 ingredients in a bowl and mix well. Then form hockey puck shapes and roll in the bread crumbs. Place the crab cakes in a hot pan with a small amount of olive oil. Do not overcrowd or they will not brown evenly. Flip each cake over after 2 to 3 minutes or when golden brown. Serve with Saffron Aioli. (See recipe below.)

Saffron Aioli
10 each saffron threads*
3 tablespoons water
½ cup mayonnaise
1 tablespoon whole grain mustard

Place Saffron threads and water in a pan and slowly bring to a simmer to extract the flavor and color from the Saffron. Combine mayonnaise and mustard in a small bowl and mix together. Add the Saffron reduction with the threads and mix completely.

(* Saffron is the dried stigma of the crocus flower and the ingredient that gives paella and curry their yellow color.) (www.wisegeek.org)

Goat Cheese and Spinach Stuffed Chicken Breast Carmelized Maui Onion Rice

1 chicken breast
1 ounce fresh spinach
3 ounces goat cheese
4 slices bacon
Salt and pepper

Preheat oven to 425 degrees. Butterfly chicken breast, flatten and salt and pepper. Place fresh spinach on top of the chicken breast then place goat cheese atop the spinach. Roll the chicken back to its original shape. Wrap the slices of bacon around the chicken and sear in a hot saucepan. Place in oven for 10 minutes or until the roll is registering 170 degrees internal temperature.

Caramelized Maui Onion Rice:
4 cups chicken stock (preferably homemade)
6 tablespoons unsalted butter (¾ stick)
1 sweet onion (Maui if you can find it)
1½ cups Arborio rice*
½ cup dry white wine
1 teaspoon kosher salt
½ teaspoon freshly ground black pepper
⅔ cup freshly grated Parmesan cheese, plus extra for serving

Place the chicken stock in a small sauce pan and bring to a simmer. In a heavy-bottomed pot or Dutch oven, melt the butter and sauté the onion over medium to low heat for 10 minutes or until caramelized. Add the rice and stir to coat the rice grains with butter.

Add the wine and cook for 2 minutes. (Reserve a portion of the wine reduction.) Add 2 full ladles of the chicken stock mixture to the rice plus the salt and pepper. Stir and simmer over low heat until the stock is absorbed, about 5 to 10 minutes. Continue to add the stock mixture, 2 ladles at a time, stirring every few minutes. Each time, cook until the mixture seems a little dry before adding more of the stock mixture. Continue until the rice is al dente (cooked fully but not soft), about 25 minutes. When finished, the rice should be thick and creamy. Place the rice on the plate, lay the chicken over the rice or on the side and top with the a sprinkle of Parmesan cheese. Enjoy!

(* Arborio is a pearly white, high starch, short grain rice that becomes creamy when cooked because it undergoes less milling than ordinary long grain rice so it retains more of its natural starch content.) (Rice Grain of Life. Wandering Wok Tours.)

Strawberry Shortcake

Buttermilk Biscuits:
8 tablespoons butter, ice cold
2 cups all-purpose flour
½ teaspoon baking soda
1½ teaspoons baking powder
1 teaspoon salt
¾ cup buttermilk

Preheat oven to 475 degrees. Slice the butter and place on a plate in the freezer. Sift the dry ingredients together into a bowl. Cut the butter into the dry ingredients with a pastry cutter or a fork until it looks like coarse sand. Add the buttermilk and continue to cut the dough together. Turn out onto a floured surface and gently form a round ball. Press the dough into a rectangle until it is between ½ and ¾ inch thick. Use a round cutter that has been floured to cut the biscuits and then place the biscuits in the freezer for at least 20 minutes. Remove from the freezer and place on parchment paper on a baking sheet so they are barely touching each other. Bake for 20 minutes.

The Filling:
1 pint strawberries, sliced
2 tablespoons sugar

Place sliced strawberries and sugar in a bowl and toss to coat. Let stand for 5 to 10 minutes or until the natural juices are released. Place on cooled baked cakes.

Homemade Whipped Cream:
2 cups heavy whipping cream

Wisk the cream until stiff peeks are formed. Chill. Place a dollop on top of the strawberry cakes.

THE SHORT STORY
Brasserie

Tom's Ice Cream Bowl

Zanesville, OH

532 McIntire Avenue
Zanesville, OH 43701
(740) 452-5267
www.tomsicecreambowl.com

Tom's has been serving its rich and creamy homemade ice cream since 1948. Not only has the shop established a reputation in the region, but it has earned national recognition by being one of *USA Today's* "10 Great Places in America to Get a Scoop." It was also listed in "The Best of Country" in *Country Living Magazine* as one of the best roadside places for sweet treats, and it is regularly mentioned in *Ohio Magazine* as one of Ohio's Best Ice Cream places.

The ambiance of this old fashioned ice cream parlor takes visitors back in time from the moment they enter this quaint place in the town of Zanesville until they leave with a creamy smile on their faces.

Owner Bill Sullivan has made sure that there is something for everyone by creating a wide variety of flavors, some that seem out of this world. All are churned on location and Bill features special flavors to compliment each season of the year. If you are an ice cream lover, this is a must place to visit on your next trip through eastern Ohio, or put it on your Bucket List.

Following are a couple confectionaries that you can make at home, but stop by Tom's and pick up a couple of pints or a gallon to assure the recipes are as delicious as you can get at Tom's.

Old Fashioned Banana Split Sundaes

½ ounce crushed maraschino cherries with juice
½ ounce crushed pineapple with juice
½ ripe banana
Tom's Ice Cream Bowl vanilla ice cream
Tom's Ice Cream Bowl chocolate ice cream
Tom's Ice Cream Bowl strawberry ice cream
1 ounce marshmallow crème
Crushed nuts (optional)

Combine crushed maraschino cherries and crushed pineapple in a small bowl and set aside. Slice the banana in the bottom of a soup bowl. On top of the banana, place 1 large scoop of vanilla ice cream. Place a slightly smaller scoop of chocolate ice cream on top of the vanilla and an even slightly smaller scoop of strawberry ice cream on top of the chocolate scoop. Add the cherry and pineapple mixture on top of the ice cream. Finally, top with marshmallow cream and, if desired, crushed nuts.

Tin Roof Sundae

Tom's Ice Cream Bowl vanilla ice cream
1 ounce chocolate syrup
1 tablespoon whole Spanish peanuts (salted)

In a soup bowl, place 2 large scoops of vanilla ice cream. Top the ice cream with your favorite chocolate syrup and whole Spanish peanuts.

Old Fashioned Ice Cream Soda

1 ounce chocolate syrup
1 ounce whole milk
16½ ounces soda water
Tom's Ice Cream Bowl vanilla ice cream

Combine chocolate syrup and milk in the bottom of a 22-ounce tumbler. Fill the tumbler with soda water and stir. Drop one scoop of vanilla ice cream into the mixture. Place another scoop of vanilla ice cream on the rim of the tumbler. If necessary, add additional soda water until the tumbler is full. Have fun with a variety of syrup and ice cream combinations.

Warehouse Steak n' Stein

Coshocton, OH

400 North Whitewoman Street
Roscoe Village
Coshocton, OH 43812
(740) 622-4001
www.warehousesteaknstein.com

As the name implies, this is a warehouse restaurant that was built in 1831 in Roscoe Village, about the time when the famous Ohio and Erie Canal was being dug from northern to southern Ohio. This building has had many uses over the years; first as a storage building for goods being transported on the Canal and eventually as a restaurant.

Owner John Larsen is responsible for completely restoring all three floors of this massive building and creating a lovely and relaxing setting where one can enjoy the latest sports programs in the tavern, be entertained by a well known comedian in the Comedy Club or listen to popular music on the patio. It's certainly worth a visit and while you are at it, spend some time browsing through the many unique and locally owned shops in the Village.

Roscoe Salad

This is a popular traditional Warehouse salad, so the preparer determines the amounts of each ingredient according to taste and number of people to be served. Mix tender mixed greens with toasted pecans, sliced pears, crumbled Bleu cheese, tart cherries and our house made Raspberry Vinaigrette. (See following recipe.)

Raspberry Vinaigrette Dressing

John hesitated to share his house Raspberry Vinaigrette dressing because it is understandably a "trade secret," but I wanted to include my easy recipe to compliment his special Warehouse salad, so here it is.

½ cup apple cider vinegar
½ cup Balsamic vinegar
2 teaspoons Dijon mustard

4 teaspoons white sugar
1 cup raspberries
½ cup vegetable oil

Combine all ingredients in a blender and mix, except the oil. Slowly add the oil and continue to blend until the mixture is smooth. Place in a glass container and store in the refrigerator. Use on salads, vegetables and meats.

Bean Soup

2 pounds dry Great Northern Beans, soaked overnight
1 large onion, chopped
3 celery stocks, chopped
3 medium carrots, diced
2 tablespoons granulated garlic
2 tablespoons granulated onion
1 tablespoon black pepper
3 tablespoons Italian seasoning
3 whole bay leaves
Pinch of thyme
1 ham hock
1 pound smoked ham, diced
3 tablespoons ham base
3 tablespoons chicken base
Water as needed

Sauté onion, celery, carrots and garlic in a pot until soft. Mix in the seasoning, herbs, ham hock and smoked ham. In a jar combine the ham base and chicken base with water and shake until they are dissolved then add to the pot. Rinse the beans in a colander and when drained add to the pot along with enough water to cover the ingredients plus about two inches above them. Cook until the beans are tender, and add more water if necessary.

CENTRAL EAST

SOUTH WEST REGION

Bacall's Café — Cincinnati, OH

Bangkok Palace — Chillicothe, OH

Beaugard's Southern BBQ — Wilmington, OH

Cruisers Diner — Seaman, OH

Dock at Water — Chillicothe, OH

The General Denver Hotel — Wilmington, OH

Golden Lamb Restaurant and Inn — Lebanon, OH

La Cascada — Hillsboro, OH

Lake White Club — Waverly, OH

Los Mariachis — Chillicothe, OH

Moyer's Winery and Restaurant — Manchester, OH

Murphin Ridge Inn — West Union, OH

Old Canal Smoke House — Chillicothe, OH

Old Y Restaurant — Winchester, OH

The Portsmouth Brewing Company — Portsmouth, OH

The Scioto Ribber — Portsmouth, OH

Spillway Lodge — Clarksville, OH

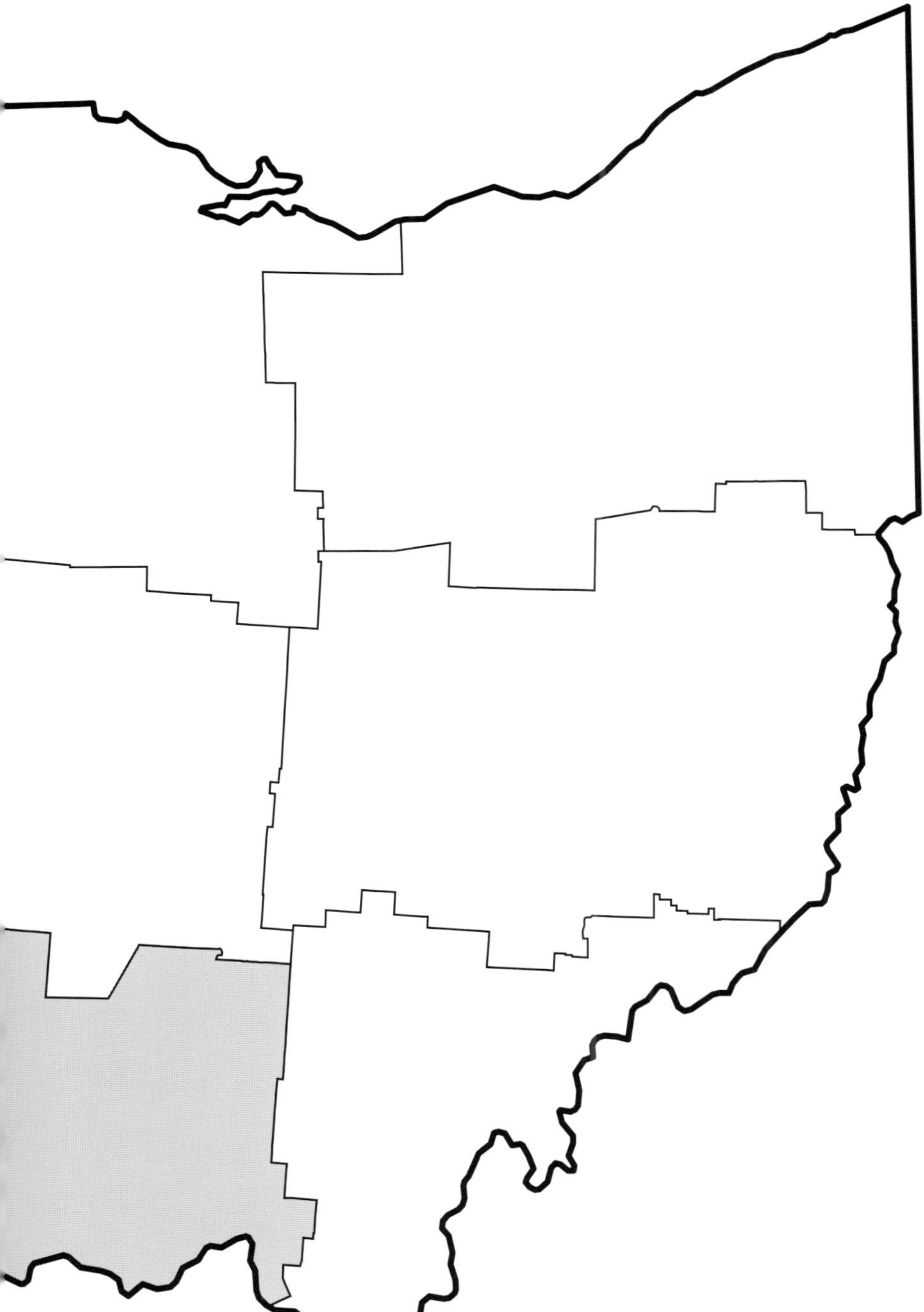

Bacall's Cafe

Cincinnati, OH

6118 Hamilton Avenue
Cincinnati, OH 45224
(513) 541-8804
www.bacallscafe.com

There are many restaurants in Cincinnati that offer a wide variety of choices for a hungry traveler, but I found Bacall's to be a diverse upscale spot located on the city's east side out of the way of the busy city and hectic traffic. However, parking is at a premium so be prepared to walk if you can't find a place nearby.

The restaurant offers diversity for its patrons. For those who are interested in sports the televisions on the bar side focus on keeping up with the latest scores and games. For those interested in enjoying the café's ambiance, the cozy dining room offers background music and a quieter atmosphere so that one can hold a conversation with friends.

A complete menu is offered on both sides of the divider starting with tasty appetizers like Wisconsin Cheese Soup, Blackened Chicken Quesadillas, and Southwestern Spring Rolls. Main entrees include the Chicken Parmesan, Beer-Battered Cod or New York Strip Steak.

Following are just a couple of their specialty recipes.

Bacall's Café White French Poppy Seed Dressing

1/8 cup chopped white onion
1 cup sugar
2/3 cup white vinegar
1 teaspoon dry mustard
1 teaspoon salt
2 cups vegetable oil
1 tablespoon poppy seeds

This is the house dressing. Combine onion, sugar, vinegar, mustard and salt in a blender and mix for at least two minutes. Slowly add vegetable oil and blend for another two minutes. Stir in poppy seeds by hand and mix well. Serve on salads or any dish for an extra punch of flavor. Store in a glass container in the refrigerator.

Bacalls Café's Cashew Chicken Salad

5 pounds white meat of chicken, diced
4 ribs of celery, finely diced
3 cups raisins
3 cups cashews, chopped
Mayonnaise
Salt
Lettuce
Tomatoes

Mix together chicken, celery, raisins, and cashews thoroughly. Add enough mayonnaise to coat and moisten. Salt to taste. Serve on a bed of lettuce and garnish with tomato slices.

Bangkok Palace

Chillicothe, OH

870 North Bridge Street
Chillicothe, OH 45601
(740) 773-8424
www.bangkokpalace45601.com

My family has been enjoying this restaurant for more than two decades. We have always admired the multiple generations of the Jauruwanakorn family who have been dedicated to serving the best oriental food this side of the Mississippi. Whenever I visit another oriental restaurant, I always compare the quality of their food to Bangkok's and find that nothing compares. The names of the entrees and dishes may be the same elsewhere, but the preparation, taste and presentation are significantly different.

My husband John's favorites are Pad Thai and Moo Goo Gai Pan, but I prefer the Triple Crown that features shrimp, crab, and scallops blended in a lobster sauce with stir fried veggies, served over fried or steamed white rice. The taste of the combination of rich seafood explodes in my mouth. It is absolutely delicious.

Owner Chai Jauruwanakorn and his wife Kristina have created a comfortable place where window shopping is encouraged through the large windows that give patrons a birds eye view of the many stores located on Bridge Street. This is a heavily travelled area so care should be taken when entering and exiting the parking lot.

I encourage you to try the following recipes at home, but, by all means, stop by Bangkok Palace for the Real Thing!

Pad Thai

8 10-ounces thin Thai-style rice noodles
2 eggs, fried
1 to 1½ cups meat – cooked chicken breast or thigh meat, or beef or shrimp
4 garlic cloves, minced
1 tablespoon white vinegar
4 to 5 green onions, chopped
3 cups dried bean sprouts
Water
½ tablespoon sugar
½ teaspoon fish salt, available where Thai food is sold

½ teaspoon MSG
Peanuts, chopped
Dried shrimp
Lime juice

Cook rice noodles in water until almost tender but not too soft. Drain, rinse and set aside. Add slightly fried eggs in a wok and steam along with chopped cooked chicken, whole shrimp or beef chunks. Mix in garlic. Steam all together over medium heat.

Add the cooked noodles to the wok for a couple of minutes Add white vinegar and shake to evenly distribute the vinegar on the noodles. Chop green onion and add to noodles and mix well.

Soak dried bean sprouts in water until semi-tender. Add to the noodles, egg and meat. To complete the cooking process, steam until noodles are soft. Add sugar, fish salt and MSG. Mix all together, add to the mixture in the wok and cook for about 5 seconds. Top with chopped peanuts mixed with dried shrimp and drizzle with lime juice to finish.

Kai Pad Cashew Chicken

4 to 5 tablespoons vegetable oil
½ cup roasted unsalted cashews
1 cup large raw chicken breasts, diced
2 tablespoons soy sauce
2 tablespoons fish sauce
2 teaspoons sugar
2 cups whole onions, cut into 1 inch squares
1 teaspoon garlic
½ bunch green onions, diced
1 tablespoon flour

In a wok, heat oil and stir fry cashews being careful not to burn them. Set aside. Add chicken to the wok until cooked. Then add soy sauce, fish sauce, sugar, onion chunks and garlic. Combine the cashews and the chicken mixture and green onions. Thicken the sauce with the flour and adjust the taste by adding additional sugar or soy sauce to counterbalance the taste of the fish sauce if it is too strong. May be served with steamed or fried rice. Serves 4 to 5.

Beaugard's Southern BBQ

Wilmington, OH

975 S. South Street
Wilmington, OH 45177
(937) 655-8100
www.beaugardsbbq.com

If you have fond memories of family picnics with grandma's old fashioned potato salad, mom's cook all day brown sugar baked beans, and Uncle Joe's spicy barbecue sauce then Beaugard's is the place to revive those great tastes of summer.

When owner Marty Beaugard retired from the Air Force years ago, he took over the family business and continued the southern tradition of smoking all meats on site which was established by his parents. This time tested process results in the meat being so tender that it falls apart. But this is an acquired skill and one that takes time and care in order to perfect just the right method. Marty was a natural and accomplished this feat with flying colors.

Of course, every good southern meal should include Sweet Potato Pie and a healthy helping of Banana Pudding. Marty has provided these delicious recipes for you to enjoy.

Sweet Potato Pie

3 medium yams
1 stick butter
1 can sweetened condensed milk
Pinch of cinnamon
Pinch of nutmeg
1 large egg
1 pre-cooked pie crust

Preheat oven to 350 degrees. Peel and boil yams until soft. Mash with butter in a medium sized bowl. Add all remaining ingredients and mix on low speed until thoroughly blended. Pour into the pie crust.

Bake for 55 to 60 minutes for one thick 9-inch pie or 35 to 45 minutes for two 8-inch pies. When done, the pie center should have a brownish color and be firm when touched.

Banana Pudding

Bananas
Vanilla Wafers
2 cans evaporated milk
½ teaspoon vanilla
1 large egg
Sugar

Alternate layers of sliced bananas and vanilla wafers in a dessert casserole dish. Set aside. Thoroughly beat an egg in a medium saucepan. Add evaporated milk and vanilla. Cook on low heat stirring constantly. When mixture starts to warm add a small amount of sugar at a time until sweetened to taste. Pudding will thicken as it heats; make sure to stir continually so it doesn't scorch. Pudding is done when it is a slightly thick consistency. Pour over banana cookie mixture. Serve either warm or chilled. Enjoy!

Cruisers Diner

Seaman, OH

155 Stern Drive
Seaman, OH 45679
(937) 386-3330
Check them out on Facebook

This stainless steel rocket diner is hard to miss and a great place to stop if you are on State Route 32 between Cincinnati and Athens. Designed and decorated in the classic 1950s theme, its authenticity does not stop with the décor, but is carried over to the menu as well. Old fashioned breakfast, lunch and dinner specials are offered daily and feature Hot Ham and Cheese, Beef and Noodles, Fried Chicken, and Mac 'n Cheese. But their desserts are simply out of this world. They seem to call your name from a clear glass display case prominently located at the entrance so that you can't miss them as you walk in the door. There are pies of all kinds from Cream and Chocolate to Apple and Berry as well as cakes and other treats.

I was able to secure not only their recipe for their delicious home style meatloaf, but also their creamy Coconut Pie.

Cruisers Meatloaf

10 pounds ground beef
7½ cups oats
5 cups onions, diced
4 cups tomato sauce
6 eggs, beaten
1¾ cups ketchup
2 tablespoons salt
1 tablespoon pepper
Cooking spray

Preheat the oven to 350 degrees. Combine beef, oats, onion, tomato sauce, eggs, ketchup, salt and pepper. Mix well and form a ball. Turn the ball onto a cutting board and knead it until firm and all ingredients are blended. Divide into 7 separate balls and form a loaf from each. Line the loaf pans with foil and spray with cooking spray.

Put a loaf in each pan and cover with foil. Bake for 1 hour and 20 minutes. Test for doneness by slicing the middle of a loaf. If the juice is clear then the loaves are done. Makes 7 loaves. Can be frozen if wrapped in foil and placed in freezer bags.

Coconut Pie

$^2/_3$ cup sugar
3 tablespoons cornstarch
2 cups milk
3 eggs, separated
1 teaspoon real vanilla
2 tablespoons butter
1 cup coconut
Pre-cooked pie crust

Preheat oven to 300 degrees. Mix sugar and cornstarch together. Add beaten egg yolks and milk and blend thoroughly. Combine the vanilla and softened butter and add to the sugar mixture. In a separate bowl beat the egg whites into firm peaks, and gently fold into the rest of the ingredients. Cook the mixture until it comes to a full boil stirring constantly. Cool then add coconut and mix well. Pour into a pie shell and bake for 1 hour or until a toothpick comes out clean.

Dock at Water

Chillicothe, OH

80 East Water Street
Chillicothe, OH 45601
(740) 779-3625
Check them out on Facebook

This local watering hole is the Cheers of Chillicothe because I see the same faces and people when I stop by and they are from all walks of life.

Located in the heart of downtown, this expansive establishment has seating at the bar, on the covered patio, or in a quiet corner in the main dining room. The atmosphere is pretty subdued during the day, but it comes to life at night when live music is often featured. The smell of freshly made popcorn hangs in the air and beverages are tall and cool. This is a great place to gather and catch up with friends.

The menu offers a variety of favorites from deep fried veggies and wings to steaks, burgers and sandwiches. This is one of my favorite places to just to chill out and relax, especially since their prices are very reasonable. I can enjoy an evening out without having to refinance my house!

Blackened Chicken Quesadillas

Blackened Seasoning:

2 teaspoons paprika, ground
4 teaspoons leaf thyme, dried
2 teaspoons onion powder
2 teaspoons garlic powder
1 teaspoon granulated sugar
2 teaspoons salt
2 teaspoons black pepper
1 teaspoon cayenne pepper, ground
1 teaspoon leaf oregano, dried
¾ teaspoon cumin, ground
½ teaspoon nutmeg, ground

For the seasoning, combine all ingredients and mix well. Place in a jar with a secure lid and store in a cool dark place.

1 chicken breast, about 8 ounces
1 tablespoon cooking oil
½ cup red onion, chopped
¼ cup Chipotle sauce
½ cup tomatoes, chopped
Lettuce

2 floured tortillas
8 ounces Cheddar cheese, shredded
Salsa (optional)
Sour cream (optional)

Shake the chicken in a bag with the blackened seasoning or pour seasoning into a bowl and coat all sides. Place on a grill and cook for about 15 minutes until tender. Dice into bite sized pieces. Heat oil in medium pan and sauté onion until transparent then add chicken pieces. Mix well. Place the chicken mixture on one tortilla and spread with cheese and Chipotle sauce. Place the other tortilla on top of the chicken, cheese and chipotle sauce. Carefully place on the grill. Toothpicks may be used to secure the quesadilla so that it does not fall apart. Grill on both sides until the cheese is melted. Serve with tomato, lettuce, salsa and sour cream.

Marinated Chicken Sandwiches

1 chicken breast, about 8 ounces
1 cup Italian dressing
1 slice Provolone cheese
Toasted bun
Lettuce
Tomato

In a small bowl, place the chicken in the Italian dressing, and cover the bowl with plastic wrap or a lid. Marinate in the refrigerator overnight. The next day, remove chicken from the dressing and drain any excess marinade. Cook over a medium hot grill until chicken is done and not pink inside. Place the cooked chicken breast on a bun and top with cheese, lettuce and tomato. Serve with chips or coleslaw.

The General Denver Hotel

Wilmington, OH

81 West Main Street
Wilmington, OH 45177
(937) 383-4141
www.generaldenver.com

In my travels I have visited many restaurants, but I am most impressed with General Denver because it is more than just a place to eat. It is a hotel or, should I say, an old fashioned inn with a number of newly refurbished rooms and an American pub in the old English tradition. There is also a large dining room that serves the overflow from the pub or the throngs that gather during the special events that regularly take place in downtown Wilmington, often organized by owner Molly Dullea.

Molly's story is quite remarkable which I related in detail in my *Eating Your Way Across Ohio* book. So suffice it to say that she is not only an entrepreneur, but a wise business woman with an eye towards increasing her business and also improving the state of the economy in this small town. A few years ago this area suffered the loss of thousands of jobs when a major employer left town. It was heartbreaking, but the unified spirit of the community adopted the attitude that they would not be defeated. Molly helped reinforce that attitude by her own determination to succeed despite the odds and that spirit has spread to others.

The architecture of the building is fascinating, but I found the food to be exquisite, clearly demonstrating the creativity of the executive chef. The following recipes give an idea of the unique possibilities using just regular ingredients.

Italian Eggs

4 farm fresh eggs, scrambled
2 tablespoons green onions
¼ cup fresh basil, chopped
2 tablespoons extra virgin olive oil
1 cup cooked egg noodles
1 tablespoons Parmesan cheese, grated
Salt and pepper
Granulated garlic

Cook scrambled eggs, green onion and basil in an oiled sauté pan until almost cooked. Add the noodles and continue to fold into the eggs as they cook. When eggs are done, fold in Parmesan cheese. Sprinkle salt, pepper and garlic to taste.

Beet Chips

2 medium beets, fresh or canned
1 teaspoon extra virgin olive oil

Preheat oven to 350 degrees. Peel beets and slice 1/16 inch thick with a mandolin slicer. In a large bowl, toss the beets with the oil. Arrange beets in a single layer on a sheet tray. Bake on the top rack until edges of beets begin to dry out, about 20 minutes. Rotate beets from the top to the bottom rack. Bake an additional 10 to 20 minutes, removing chips as they become lighter in color. Transfer chips to a wire rack where they will become crispy as they cool.

Grilled Cheese with Sauteed Greens, Scallions, and Roasted Garlic Aioli

Greens of 2 beets
1 tablespoon olive oil
1 cup green onion, sliced
Salt and pepper
8 slices of dilly bread, or other crusted bread
8 slices Mozzarella cheese

Clean and chop beet greens, discarding stem. Pan sauté greens with onions in the olive oil until just tender. Salt and pepper. Brush bread with oil and place in hot skillet oil side down. Layer bread with cheese, sauté mix and roasted garlic aioli. (See recipe below.)

Roasted Garlic Aioli
2 medium whole garlic hearts
1 tablespoon olive oil
1½ cups mayonnaise
2 teaspoons apple cider vinegar
½ teaspoon black pepper
¼ teaspoon salt

Cut off and discard tops of garlic heads to expose cloves, then brush each head with ½ tablespoon oil. Wrap heads together in foil and bake at 325 degrees until tender, about 45 minutes. Cool them until they are barely warm. Squeeze the garlic cloves from the skins into a food processor and puree with mayonnaise, vinegar, pepper and salt.

Golden Lamb Restaurant & Inn

Lebanon, OH

27 South Broadway Street
Lebanon, OH 45036
(513) 932-5065
www.goldenlamb.com

Established in 1803, the Golden Lamb is Ohio's oldest continuously operating inn. The building has greatly expanded since then, but it has maintained its charm. It has also played a significant part in history by welcoming more than 12 U.S. Presidents under its roof including James Garfield, William McKinley, John Quincy Adams, Ulysses S. Grant, Martin Van Buren, Ronald Reagan and George W. Bush. It has also been a key stop in the state where many presidential candidates choose to deliver stump speeches. Other well known names such as Charles Dickens and Mark Twain have also paid visits and enjoyed a meal in the dining room. In fact, many of the historic rooms are named after famous guests.

The main dining room features full entrees such as Roast Duck and Red Snapper Creole. But for casual fare the Black Horse Tavern offers generous man-size sandwiches and a variety of hardy soups. You will not likely forget the Golden Lamb once you have been there. It seamlessly combines the allure of a bygone era with the prevailing tastes of the 21st century.

Sister Lizzie's Shaker Sugar Pie

1/3 cup flour
1 cup brown sugar, about 3/4 of a small box
9-inch unbaked pie crust
2 cups light cream, Half and Half
1 teaspoon vanilla
2 tablespoons butter, about 4 thin pats of a stick of butter
Nutmeg

Preheat oven to 350 degrees. Mix the flour and sugar together by rubbing the dry mix back and forth between the palms of your hands.

After it is thoroughly mixed, spread evenly into the pie shell. Pour the cream and vanilla over the sugar/flour mixture but DO NOT stir (during baking it bubbles and mixes on its own). Evenly place the butter slices atop the cream, and sprinkle the entire top of pie with nutmeg.

Bake the pie for at least an hour in a conventional oven (or 40 to 45 minutes in a pizza oven*). The pie is done when it becomes firm. Another way to test for doneness is give the pan a twist back and forth, if the shell moves easily in the pan, it is done.

(*The Golden Lamb used pizza ovens frequently, and the pie pans sat directly onto the floor or base of the oven. In this style of oven the cooking time for a sugar pie is 40-45 minutes.)

Egg Salad

6 hard-boiled eggs, chopped
2 ribs of celery, chopped
1 medium red bell pepper, chopped
1 tablespoon yellow mustard
Dash of each: Tabasco sauce, white pepper, Worcestershire sauce
Salt to taste
2 tablespoons mayonnaise

Chill the eggs, celery and pepper before you chop them to a medium size, not too fine. Mix together the rest of the ingredients except mayonnaise. Finally, fold in the mayonnaise, but don't worry about thickness, it is supposed to be thick. Serve it on bread as a sandwich or with club crackers and enjoy!

Old Fashioned Potato Soup

¼ cup butter
1 cup leeks, cleaned and sliced
1 onion, peeled and chopped
1 tablespoon all purpose flour
4 cups chicken broth or 4 cups chicken stock
2 pounds potatoes, peeled and sliced
2 cups milk
2 cups Half and Half

½ teaspoon salt
¼ teaspoon pepper
⅛ teaspoon dried marjoram
⅛ teaspoon dried thyme leaves

Melt butter in a stockpot over a medium high heat. Add leeks and onions and cook until translucent. Stir in flour until well mixed and add broth or stock and bring to a boil stirring constantly. When it is slightly thickened, add potatoes and reduce heat to a simmer. Cook 20 to 25 minutes or until potatoes are tender. Add all remaining ingredients and cook until thoroughly heated.

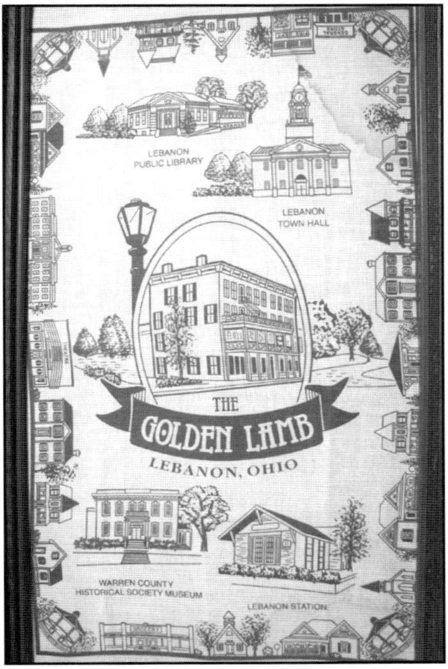
LEBANON
PUBLIC LIBRARY
LEBANON
TOWN HALL
THE
GOLDEN LAMB
LEBANON, OHIO
WARREN COUNTY
HISTORICAL SOCIETY MUSEUM
LEBANON STATION

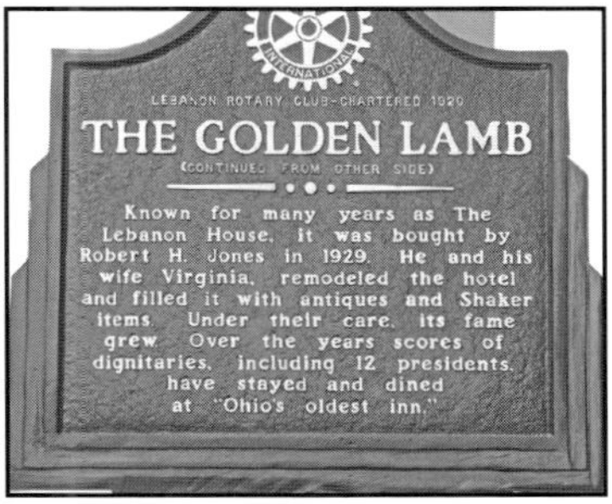
LEBANON ROTARY CLUB-CHARTERED 1920
THE GOLDEN LAMB
(CONTINUED FROM OTHER SIDE)
Known for many years as The Lebanon House, it was bought by Robert H. Jones in 1929. He and his wife Virginia, remodeled the hotel and filled it with antiques and Shaker items. Under their care, its fame grew. Over the years scores of dignitaries, including 12 presidents, have stayed and dined at "Ohio's oldest inn."

La Cascada

Hillsboro, OH

140 Roberts Lane
Hillsboro, OH 45133
(937) 393-8861
www.lacascadamexicancuisine.com

I eat at La Cascada as often as possible when I am in Hillsboro especially on days when I'm teaching on the local campus of Southern State Community College. The restaurant is clean and colorful and located in a convenient part of town with plenty of parking.

After I visited the first time I discovered that the same owners have other locations in Lancaster, Logan, and Marysville and I have tried them as well. The location may be different, but the menus are the same in each location.

Tortilla Chips with Salsa

12 10-inch tortillas, corn or flour
Oil
Salsa, bottled or prepared from recipe below

Lay tortilla shells on a flat surface and cut each into 8 equal triangular pieces. Pour ½ inch of oil in a skillet and heat until hot but not smoking. Fry tortillas until crisp, turning one time. Remove from skillet and lay on paper towels to drain. Serve warm with salsa.

Salsa:
2 large tomatoes, peeled, seeded and chopped
½ medium onion, chopped
1 4-ounce can diced green chilies
½ teaspoon garlic salt
½ teaspoon oregano
Salt to taste

Place all ingredients in a bowl and gently stir together. Let the salsa sit at room temperature for at least 1 hour so that all the flavors can blend before serving. Makes about 2 cups.

Nachos

6 cups homemade tortilla chips
1½ cups grated Cheddar or Monterey Jack cheese
1 or 2 jalapeno chilies, finely chopped
Sour cream
Black olives

Preheat oven to 400 degrees. Prepare the tortilla chips according to the recipe provided. Spread about 2 cups of chips in a flat baking pan. Top with a ½ cup of cheese and 1/3 of the chilies. Layer another 2 cups of the chips, cheese and chilies. Repeat again.

Bake until cheese is melted, about 10 minutes. Garnish with sour cream and several black olives, if desired. Serve immediately. Makes 6 servings.

Tacos

This is a quick and easy meal, where everyone makes their own once the ingredients are prepared.

12 taco shells, crisp or soft
Lettuce, shredded
Tomatoes, diced
Taco sauce
Cheddar or Monterey Jack, grated
Sour cream
Beef filling or sausage and cheese filling

Arrange taco shells on a plate as well as lettuce, tomatoes, taco sauce, cheese, and sour cream separately along with one or both of the fillings: beef or sausage and cheese.

Beef Filling:
2 tablespoons oil
1 medium onion, chopped
1 pound lean ground beef
½ cup enchilada sauce

Heat oil in a skillet and sauté the onion until transparent. Add ground meat and cook until lightly brown. Break apart into small pieces. Stir in the sauce and cook over low heat for about 10 minutes, stirring to blend completely. Makes about 2 cups.

Sausage and Cheese Filling:
¾ Mexican Chorizo sausage or pork sausage
A dash cayenne pepper
½ pound Monterey Jack cheese

Remove the casing from the sausage and chop it into small chunks. In a heavy skillet cook for about 15 to 20 minutes until brown. Pour off the grease. Makes about 2 cups.

Putting it Together:
Select a taco shell and place a strip of filling of choice along the middle of the shell. Add lettuce, tomatoes, and taco sauce. Top with sour cream and cheese to make an easy meal. Serve with guacamole and sour cream.

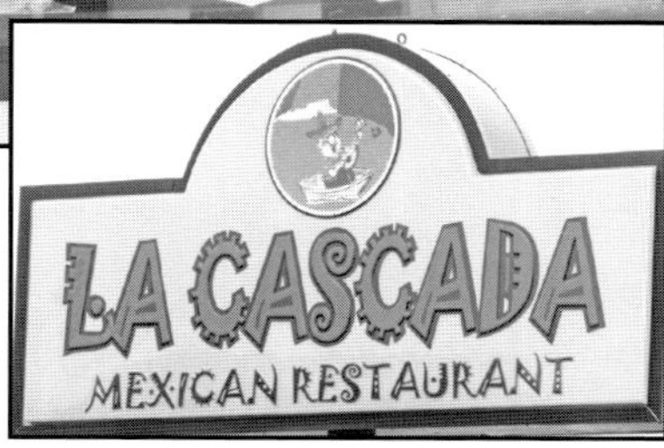

SOUTH WEST

Lake White Club

Waverly, OH

1166 State Route 552
Waverly, OH 45690
(740) 947- 5000
(800) 774-LAKE
www.lakewhiteclub.com

The Lake White Club was established in the 1930s and soon became an Ohio playground for visitors around the state and even for a few governors. Originally, the structure was a log cabin built in the 1820s, but it underwent numerous transitions to eventually become the building that houses this picturesque restaurant today.

A few years ago, ownership changed hands and a general face lift began to transform the age old structure to a more attractive and welcoming place overlooking the lake. Open all year round, it is certainly a fun place where you can enjoy your friends and good food.

The Lake White Club has always been known for its tender Fried Chicken and thinly sliced breaded Onion Rings, but the steaks are made to order and the fresh seafood is broiled or fried to perfection. Each table is served family style beginning with appetizers and finishing with delectable desserts like Post Mortem. No, this is not your state of being after the meal, but a concoction that is so scrumptious it is deadly, figuratively speaking, of course!

The view of the Lake is relaxing and the surrounding area is beautiful during all four seasons of the year. In warmer weather, the Lake is dotted with boaters and swimmers, but during the colder months, the winged wild life take over. Whatever the time of year, it is a great place to catch a good meal, drink in the atmosphere and observe Mother Nature at her best.

Since business has picked up in the last year or so, it is advisable to call ahead for reservations and their new hours. Though during the week, walk-ins are usually seated fairly quickly.

Bacon and Bleu Cheese Steak Salad

10 ounce flat iron chuck steak
Cajun seasoning
Fresh baby spinach
1 red onion
Bleu cheese crumbles
Sweet hot bacon dressing

Season flat iron steak with Cajun seasoning and grill to medium rare or medium and slice thin. Toss baby spinach with thinly sliced red onion, Bleu cheese crumbles, and dressing. Place spinach mixture on plate and place sliced steak on top of spinach. Top with additional Bleu cheese crumbles for garnish.

Mahi Mahi Fish Tacos

Cilantro Lime Sour Cream

3 cups sour cream
¼ cup fresh cilantro
Juice from 1 lime

In a small mixing bowl, combine sour cream, fresh cilantro and juice from 1 lime. Mix thoroughly and set aside.

Caribbean Vegetable Slaw

1 zucchini
1 yellow squash
1 red pepper
1 red onion
Sweet Caribbean Dressing, Kraft or Marzetti
Salt and pepper

Julienne zucchini, yellow squash, red pepper and red onion. Toss in a bowl with sweet Caribbean dressing. Salt and pepper to taste.

Putting it Together:

6 to 8 ounces Mahi Mahi
Cajun Seasoning
1 cup uncooked rice
2 cups chicken broth
3 flour tortilla shells
4 ounces green peas
2 ounces vegetable slaw

Cut Mahi Mahi into strips and season with Cajun seasoning. Sauté the fish strips in a hot skillet until they are cooked thoroughly and flakey. Cook rice in the chicken broth according to directions on the box. Place flour tortilla shells on a plate and divide the Mahi Mahi on each tortilla. Top with 1 ounce of the vegetable slaw on each strip and garnish each taco with the Cilantro Lime Sour Cream mixture. Serve with a scoop of rice and peas on the side.

Los Mariachis

Chillicothe, OH

646 Central Center
Chillicothe, OH 45601
(740) 775-1403

1080 North Bridge Street
Chillicothe, OH 45601
(740) 775-4219

Check them out on Facebook

This is a fun upbeat place where the food is tasty and the atmosphere is charged with energy. My husband and I often have New Year's Eve dinner here with friends, and we particularly enjoy the genuine Mariachi Band that sets the tone for the whole evening. As they strum and sing, we hum along and enjoy the harmony of their combined voices. It is like being in Acapulco.

I have always been impressed with the efficiency of the servers here. Chips and salsa are on the table as you arrive and refilled frequently. The entrees are authentic Mexican cuisine with generous portions that are hot off the grill, sometimes still sizzling as they are delivered to the table. Wine and beer are available, but the Margaritas, served in large fish bowl size glasses, quench the thirst after a basket of chips.

Most of the time, the televisions positioned around the restaurant are tuned to Spanish speaking programs or sports. Either way there is always entertainment.

Since the *Eating Your Way Across Ohio* book was published, a second Los Mariachis location has opened, but the menus for both locations are the same. If you enjoy Mexican cuisine, you won't be disappointed here. It is also a good place to practice your Spanish since most of the servers speak very little English.

Guacamole

2 large ripe avacados
2 to 3 tablespoons lemon or lime juice
1 small clove of garlic, minced
1 tablespoon fresh cilantro, chopped
1 medium tomato, seeded and chopped
1 can of green chilies, rinse, seeded and chopped

3-4 tablespoons sour cream
Salt and pepper

Cut open the avocados length wise and scoop out the avocado pulp and place in a medium bowl. Discard the shells. Mash the pulp by hand with a fork and add lemon or lime juice, garlic, cilantro, tomato and chilies and mix together. Blend in the sour cream to give the mixture a creamy texture. Serve with most any Mexican dish.

Taco Salad

This is the traditional taco salad served cold and in a taco shell with either beef or chicken. The second recipe is a warm taco salad which is a different spin on this favorite dish.

4 to 6 large salad taco shells
1 pound ground beef or cooked spicy chicken
1 package of taco sauce
3 to 4 cups lettuce, chopped
2 medium tomatoes, chopped
Melted cheese sauce
4 cups guacamole
2 cups chicken broth
Ranch dressing

Taco shells can easily be made with the help of the non-stick taco shell makers that come in 6 and 8 inch sizes. Soft tortillas are placed in the mold and are either deep fried or baked until crisp. Follow the cooking times on the package. After cooking, place on wax paper to cool and as the shells dry they become firm. In the meantime, brown the beef or heat the chicken in a skillet over medium heat. Mix in taco sauce until it is blended with the meat. Place lettuce and tomato in the taco shell, follow with the beef or chicken mixture, and top with cheese sauce. Serve with guacamole and ranch dressing on the side.

Taco Salad Fajita

Unlike the above taco salad, this one is served warm in a soft tortilla. There is an obvious difference in the preparation and the taste of each.

1 pound ground beef or 1 pound of chicken, white and dark meat, shredded
2 tablespoons of olive oil

1 onion, chopped
1 large bell pepper, chopped
2 medium tomatoes, chopped
½ cup lettuce
Soft tortilla shell
¾ cup Monterey Jack cheese, shredded
½ cup black olives, sliced
Guacamole sauce

Pour oil in a skillet and brown ground meat. If chicken is desired, cook until it is cooked thoroughly. Add the onion and peppers, and cook until tender but not too soft. They should still be a little crunchy. Stir in tomatoes and lettuce and cook for 3 to 5 minutes longer. Cover and remove from the heat. Place mixture in a soft tortilla and top with cheese and black olives. Serve with a side of guacamole.

Moyer's Winery and Restaurant

Manchester, OH

3859 U.S. Rt. 52
Manchester, OH 45144
(937) 549-2957
http://www. moyerwinery
restaurant.com/About-Us.html

Located along U.S. 52 between Cincinnati and Manchester, this is an absolutely charming and elegant restaurant overlooking the Ohio River, However, you might need a GPS to find it. Just look for the quaint 1920s era building amidst the acres of vineyards.

During its long history the building has served as a dance hall, boxing site, private gambling club and truck stop, Ken and Mary Moyer purchased this vintage building in 1973. Their menu at that time consisted of bean soup, cheese, and French bread accompanied by regular wine tastings from the fruit of Ken's limited crop of grapes and processed by his newly acquired skill of wine-making. It was a rough start but Ken and Mary persevered and the restaurant grew along with its reputation.

In 1999, the Moyers sold the restaurant and winery to a group of friends with the promise they would maintain its distinctive reputation. Over the years the menu expanded to feature a wide selection of appetizers, such as breaded and deep Fried Chicken Livers, Pan-Blackened Chicken, and Salmon Steaks nestled in a mound of creamy rich mashed potatoes garnished with hollandaise sauce and covered with freshly steamed asparagus.

Ken expanded his selection of wines by cultivating an increasing assortment of grapes, like Vidal Blanc grapes used for white wines, and DeChaunac and Chambourcin grapes used for his red wines. To make sure he captured the best taste from his crop, he had the grapes pressed the very day of harvest. All processing and bottling still takes place on the lower level of the building beneath the restaurant, which has been updated and is now a modern facility. Ken's processing procedure is still followed today which has resulted in Moyers becoming an award winning winery producing 30,000 bottles each year.

The sign hanging by the door invites hungry travelers to: "*Come, Relax and Enjoy*," which is so easy to do here!

Moyer's Cream Cheese Dip

This is Ken's favorite appetizer and I can understand why. It has a nutty cheesy flavor that compliments salty or fruity flavors.

24 ounces cream cheese, soft
2 cups Bleu cheese crumbles
¾ cup pecans
1½ teaspoons Tabasco sauce

Place cream cheese in a small mixing bowl and beat until creamy. Add Bleu cheese, pecans and Tabasco and continue to blend the ingredients until mixed well. Serve with fruit and crackers.

Lemon Pie

2 lemons, grated
Juice of 2 lemons
8 ounces of Cool Whip
4 cans of Eagle Brand Sweetened Condensed Milk
½ cup lemonade concentrate
½ teaspoon yellow food coloring
2 8-inch graham cracker pie crusts

Place the grated peel of the lemons, the lemon juice, and Cool Whip in a medium sized stainless steel bowl. Mix well then increase the speed.

Slowly add the milk one can at a time. Then add the lemonade concentrate and food coloring, blending at high speed until thick and peaks are formed. The mixture should easily pull away from the bowl and when the frost decreases on the side of the mixing bowl the mixture is done.

Spoon equal amounts into each pie crust and garnish with a lemon peel twist on top.

Murphin Ridge Inn

West Union, OH

750 Murphin Ridge Road
West Union, OH 45693
(877) 687-7446
(937) 544-2263
www.murphinridgeinn.com

Not too far from Moyer's Winery, high on top of one of Adam County's highest hills, sits Murphin Ridge nestled neatly into the countryside. It is quite a surprise to find this 140 acre resort located seemingly in the middle of nowhere. What better place to have a secluded retreat, than at the end of a winding road and far away from the chaotic world below.

After former owners Darryl and Sherry McKenney purchased the primitive 1820s farmhouse, they converted it into a rustic restaurant. Then they proceeded to build nine woodland cabins with modern facilities to cater to the creature comforts of their guests.

Murphin Ridge not only provides privacy, but it also offers all the amenities that one might expect from a get away like this: vast fields for long walks, comfortable cabins for lounging, an abundance of wild life to observe, large gardens to admire and excellent homemade cuisine to savor.

Seasonal items abound on the menu and are often harvested fresh from the garden. In fact, a beautiful cookbook featuring the Murphin Ridge cuisine is available, so ask to purchase a copy at their gift shop. Following are just a few samples of dishes you can order at the restaurant.

Smokehouse Salmon

The restaurant has many neighbors who cut cedar high on the hill at Murphin Ridge. They use the cedar in this deliciously simple recipe for salmon, but warn that the secret is more the freshness of the fish than what you do with it.

Fish:
1 salmon filet per person, cut 2 inches wide
Good quality olive oil

Salt and pepper to taste
Fresh lemon
Fresh dill, chopped

Preheat oven to 500 degrees. Soak your cedar plank in water for an hour so it won't burn. Brush fish on both sides with olive oil and season with salt and pepper. Brush the plank with oil as well and place the salmon on it and roast for 10 minutes per inch of thickness of salmon. (Roast a 2- inch filet for 20 minutes for well done fish; a little less time for medium or rare). Do not overcook. The salmon is done when it flakes easily. Top with freshly squeezed lemon juice and chopped dill.

Fresh Tomato Salsa
2 summer tomatoes, chopped
½ sweet onion, chopped
2 tablespoons fresh dill, chopped
2 garlic cloves, minced
2 tablespoons sugar
3 tablespoons vinegar
2 tablespoons olive oil
1 tablespoon canola oil

Mix together all the ingredients for the fresh tomato salsa and serve with the salmon. Makes 4 servings.

Chocolate Bread Pudding

This recipe is delicious year-round and is an elegant way to utilize stale bread.

Oil
8 cups Amish White bread, cut into ½-inch cubes with crust on
2½ cups heavy cream, divided
9 ounces bittersweet chocolate
1 stick unsalted butter
2 cups dried apricots, chopped
½ cup orange liquor
1 cup water
1½ cups sugar, divided
5 large eggs
½ cup flour
1½ cups almonds, chopped

Preheat oven to 350 degrees. Oil a 9 x 13 inch glass baking pan. Put the bread cubes in a large bowl and add 2 cups of the heavy cream. Let the mixture stand for 30 minutes. In a small pan over a low heat, melt the chocolate and butter with the remaining heavy cream. Stir until the chocolate is smooth, then transfer the mixture to a bowl to let it slightly cool. In the meantime, macerate (grind or crush) the apricots in the liquor and water. Stir 1 cup of the sugar into the warm chocolate mixture. Whisk in eggs one at a time. Sift the flour over the mixture and fold in thoroughly. Combine the chocolate mixture, almonds, apricots, and bread mixture, stirring until all the ingredients are thoroughly combined. Pour the mixture into the prepared pan and sprinkle it with the remaining ½ cup of sugar.

Bake 50 to 60 minutes, or until the pudding is set and a knife inserted into the middle comes out clean. Transfer the pan to a rack and let it cool. Serve with almond whipped cream. Makes 8 to 10 servings

Almond Whipped Cream
2 cups heavy whipping cream
¼ - ½ cup confectioner's sugar
1 teaspoon almond extract

Add all ingredients to a mixing bowl and whip until firm peaks form. Place a dollop on each serving of the pudding.

SOUTH WEST

Old Canal Smoke House

Chillicothe, OH

94 East Water Street
Chillicothe, OH 45601
(740) 779-3278
www.oldcanalsmokehouse.com

Since my last review of the Old Canal Smoke House, located on the corner of Water and Mulberry Streets, a major fire and change of ownership have taken place.

The former owners had to renovate much of the interior when a fire from a nearby house destroyed part of the Old Canal structure. Smoke damage was extensive, but after months of construction, the place was restored to its previous charm where guests can relax and enjoy the casual atmosphere. There is no trace of smoke or fire damage and this has once again become a favorite downtown spot where meeting with friends can be done in the attractive dining rooms or on the spacious covered patio.

The new owners, Bill and Tammy Barker and sons, Bill J. and Ryan, are a well established family of restaurateurs who own other eating places around town. They have promised that the menu will not change significantly, and that the popular Hickory Smoked Ribs, Pulled Pork and Brisket served with their unique house barbecue sauce will be a mainstay on the menu.

Armadillo Eggs

2 or 3 skinless boneless chicken breasts
3 to 4 inch jalapeno chilies
Bacon, uncooked
Old Canal Smoke House BBQ sauce
Toothpicks
Monterey Jack cheese, sliced

Preheat oven to 400 degrees. Cut raw chicken breasts in half length ways resulting in two strips about ½ inch thick. Wash, core and cut jalapenos length ways. Lay peppers along one side of the chicken breast length ways. Place the other pepper strip on the 2nd strip of meat, and sandwich the pepper between the strips. In order to hold the meat together wrap 1 or 2 pieces of bacon around it and secure with as many toothpicks necessary to prevent the meat from opening up during cooking.

Bake for 25 to 30 minutes depending on the size of the pepper and the thickness of the chicken. Remove from the oven and coat with the BBQ sauce and grill for 3 to 4 minutes. Place a slice of cheese on each piece of chicken and return to the grill for only about 1 minute to allow the cheese to melt. No eggs and no Armadillos, but a doggone good chicken dish!

Old Y Restaurant

Winchester, OH

1940 U.S. Rt. 62 South
Winchester, OH 45697
(937) 442-3222

This is a well established diner located outside of Hillsboro that has a history dating back to the 1950s. At one time the unique attraction was a full sized commercial plane that was actually attached to the main restaurant. It accommodated adventurous diners who wanted to live vicariously by dining in a plane. Over the years, despite the attention the plane drew, its deteriorating condition required it to be removed from the premises which left the restaurant on its own. Eventually, a large white gazebo replaced the plane as a landmark distinguishing The Old Y from other area eateries. Located in front of the restaurant, make sure you look for it when you are travelling down U.S. Rt. 62.

At the same time, stop in and try their delicious moist Meatloaf, homemade Chicken and Noodles, or tender Baked Steak. Finish the meal with a slice of Rhubarb Custard Pie and then use the following recipe to make one at home.

Corn Salad

Vegetables

2 cups cooked whole kernel corn, frozen or fresh
1 medium tomato, chopped
1 medium rib celery, chopped
¼ cup green onions, sliced
1 tablespoon fresh parsley, minced

Dressing

¼ cup lowfat mayonnaise,
Miracle Whip Lite works well
1 tablespoon white vinegar
½ teaspoon sugar
¾ teaspoon salt

1/8 teaspoon pepper
Lettuce
Bread bowl, optional

In a medium bowl, combine the corn, tomato, celery, onions and parsley. Mix well. In a separate small bowl mix the mayonnaise and vinegar until smooth. Add sugar, salt and pepper. Combine the vegetable mixture and the dressing. Serve in lettuce-lined bread bowls or just over a bed of lettuce.

Oatmeal Raisin Bread

½ cup whole wheat flour
½ cup firmly packed dark brown sugar
1 teaspoon salt
½ cup butter, softened
1 cup raisins
2 cups boiling water
1 package dry yeast
½ cup warm water
1 cup quick cooking oats, uncooked
5 to 6 cups all-purpose flour
½ cup sugar
1 tablespoon ground cinnamon
Melted butter or margarine

Preheat oven to 375 degrees. Combine wheat flour, brown sugar, salt, butter and raisins in a large bowl. Add 2 cups boiling water, stirring to melt the butter. Cool the mixture. Dissolve the yeast in ½ cup warm water and let stand for 5 minutes. Add to oats and mix well. Gradually stir in enough flour to make a soft dough. Turn dough out on a floured surface and knead until smooth and elastic, about 8 to 10 minutes. Place in a well greased bowl turning it in order to grease the top. Cover and let rise in a warm place free from drafts for 1 hour or until doubled in bulk.

Punch dough down, turn out on floured surface and knead 2 minutes. Divide dough in half and let rest 10 minutes. Roll each half into 9 x 18 inch rectangle. In a small bowl, combine sugar and cinnamon, and sprinkle half this mixture evenly over each rectangle. Roll jellyroll fashion beginning at short end. Fold ends under and place in two greased 9 x 5 x 3 inch loaf pans. Brush with melted butter. Cover and let rise in a warm place for 40 to 50 minutes or until doubled in size.

Bake for 40 to 45 minutes or until loaves sound hollow when tapped. Remove loaves from pans and cool on wire racks. Makes 2 loaves.

Rhubarb Custard Pie

1 pint milk
1 teaspoon flour
Water
3 eggs, beaten
½ cup sugar
Pinch of salt
2 cups rhubarb, finely chopped

Preheat oven to 400 degrees. In a medium pan heat milk on low heat until warm. In a separate bowl combine flour with enough water to make a paste. Add mixture to the warm milk and pour over the eggs and blend in the sugar and salt to form a custard. Mix well. Cover bottom of unbaked pie shell with the rhubarb. Pour custard over the rhubarb. Bake for 10 minutes being careful not to let it bubble. Reduce the heat to 350 degrees and cook another 30 minutes.

PEPSI
The Old Y
RESTAURANT

The Portsmouth Brewing Company

Portsmouth, OH

224 Second Street
Portsmouth, OH 45662
(740) 354-6106
www.portsmouthohbrewing.com

"A modern brewing tradition combining artisan craft with state of the art technology."

The history of the Portsmouth Brewing Company is quite fascinating. Established twenty years before the Civil War in 1843, it is Ohio's oldest brewery. Its reputation for beer making was met with mediocre success under various owners until Julius Esselborn, a German immigrant, purchased the brewery in 1889. He not only made major renovations to the building, combining the original structure with an adjacent one to create a more practical use of space, but he also built the business up to achieve peak production of 20,000 barrels of beer a year. Upon his death in 1890, his son, Paul, stepped into his shoes and led the company through a series of major challenges including the Flood of 1913 which it survived. Eventually, Paul became the most famous Portsmouth Brewing Company brewer, but there was trouble ahead.

The 1920s Prohibition put the Brewing Company out of business until it was purchased in 1995 by home brewers and brothers Steve and Ira Mault. Their avid interest and financial investment resurrected the popularity of brewing beer in 1997 which preserved Portsmouth's craft brewing tradition. In addition to reopening the brewery, they also updated the facility with state of the art equipment, and created a Beer Pub and a spacious Beer Garden where guests can enjoy their favorite brew in an open air setting.

Their most popular beers include the Red Bird Ale, which was the flagship beer in the early days of the brewery, as well as the Portsmouth Pilsner and the Crystal Gold Lager, which are similar to the German lagers produced by the Esselborns in the late 1800s. Other varieties that are available are the Oatmeal Stout and the Excelsior Dark Lager. They usually have Portsmouth Pilsner and Peerless Pale Ale in both bottles and on draft, but specialized and seasonal brews are also available for special occasions. To get a general idea of which beer pleases your palate, order the PBC Sampler of six beers (3 ounces each).

Of course, when you have a good brew, you need a good meal and they have that covered. A wide variety of fried appetizers are available, like Mozzarella Sticks, Pub Fries, Breaded Pickle Spears, Spinach Artichoke Dip, and Onion Rings, as well as entrees such as prime rib, steaks and chicken. Each dish can be paired with a beer of your choice.

If you enjoy historical sites and the combination of good food and craft beer, this is certainly worth a visit. At the same time, check out the nearby bigger than life murals that depict the history of the Portsmouth area.

Brewmaster Emily Uldrich shared the following recipe to give my readers an idea of what is involved in the large scale brewing process of craft beer. However, if you are inclined to try this at home, I would suggest adjusting the recipe. She also noted that this beer is not currently being produced by the brewery.

Ginger Shandy

Makes 10 BBL (beer barrels or 310 gallons) of Ginger Shandy with 2% ABV (alcohol by volume)

Malt Grist:

200 pounds Two Row Malt
10 pounds Carapils Malt
25 pounds Caramel-20 Malt

Start out by mashing all the dry ingredients in hot water for 1 hour at 151 degrees F. Sparge, or rinse the grist, to achieve 380 gallons and collect in the Brew Kettle and bring to a boil. At the beginning of the boiling process, add 20 pounds of lactose (unfermentable sugar). Boil for 1 hour, then add 10 pounds fresh pureed Ginger and boil for another 30 minutes. After cooling, add Ale Yeast for fermentation. Before bunging (ending the fermentation process which is not necessary in home brewing) add 180 ounces of Ginger Extract. After fermentation is complete cool below 40 degrees F and carbonate.

According to Emily, brewing beer at home is similar to commercial brewing. Home brewers can select from ingredients identical to those used in commercial brewing. The basic ingredients that are necessary include water, malt, hops (no hops in this recipe), and yeast.

SOUTH WEST

The Scioto Ribber

Portsmouth, OH

1026 Gallia Street
Portsmouth, OH 45662
(740) 353-9329
www.theribber.com

Located only a few blocks away, The Ribber is the sister company of the Portsmouth Brewing Company and both are owned by the Mault family. The building is unassuming from the outside. In fact, the first time I visited at night years ago, I truly wondered why we had driven hours to come to such a remote place like Portsmouth and to such an unexceptional looking place to eat.

Well, I was pleasantly surprised. First, the Ribber wasn't small at all. From the street it was quite deceptive. Once inside, I discovered that the building was very deep with multiple dining areas. Second, we could barely find a seat because it was so crowded. So I figured that it must live up to its reputation since it appeared to be so popular. And then I found out that their ribs were the most tender I had ever tasted especially when dipped in their famous homemade barbeque sauce. And their steaks are cooked to perfection.

Something else I particularly liked was that all meals came complete with potatoes, onion rings, coleslaw and choice of green beans or baked beans. Next time I won't judge a restaurant by its initial appearance. That was a few years ago and not much has changed except word has spread, and The Ribber has only become more popular.

German Coleslaw

1 medium head cabbage
Salt
½ cup vinegar
⅓ cup water
⅓ cup sugar
½ teaspoon celery seed
½ teaspoon mustard seed
½ teaspoon seasoned salt

½ green pepper, grated
½ small onion, grated

Cut cabbage into wedges and place in a large bowl. Sprinkle with salt. Let stand for 1 hour. In a small pan combine the vinegar, cold water, sugar, celery seed, mustard seed, and seasoned salt. Stir well and bring to a boil over a medium heat. Remove from heat and let cool. Add green pepper and onion to the cabbage. Then add the cooled vinegar mixture, stirring well. Refrigerate overnight in order to allow the flavors to blend together. Store long term by freezing coleslaw in individual freezer containers of any size. Label with the contents' name and date.

Spillway Lodge

Clarksville, OH

623 Old State Road
Clarksville, OH 45113
(937) 289-2168

Steve Benney who is not only the owner of The Spillway Lodge, but also the executive chef, has continued the legacy of his parents since they passed ownership to him in 1986. Steve assumed the responsibility of maintaining the fine reputation of this charming and extraordinary restaurant located on a quiet country road near Clarksville, and he hasn't wavered from that goal since.

His culinary creativity is reflected in his ability to prepare a variety of dishes, but I was particularly impressed by the exquisite seafood dishes. He starts with the largest shrimp I have ever seen, most the size of my closed fist, and fixes them in a variety of ways including scampi, stuffed, fried and grilled on skewers. He also prepares the most delicious melt in your mouth Alaskan King Crab Legs compete with drawn butter. But he doesn't ignore his beef eating customers and chooses locally grown beef, which he hand cuts into steaks and grills to order. A few of his selections are Filet Mignon, New York Strip and Chopped Sirloin garnished with mushrooms and onions. They are as tender as you would eat anywhere.

This restaurant was initially recommended to me and I have been a repeat guest. I have always been pleased with the quality of the cuisine, the attentive service and the atmosphere. It is all around enjoyable.

Spillway Ribs and BBQ Sauce

24 ounces ketchup
1 cup sugar
2 tablespoons Worcestershire Sauce
2 tablespoons chili powder
1 medium onion
¼ to ½ teaspoon garlic salt
½ teaspoon tarragon
2 tablespoons grape jelly, Welch's or Smuckers
¼ cup bourbon

Full rack of ribs, baby back loin preferably
Water

Combine all ingredients together except for the ribs and water, and process in a blender until thoroughly mixed. Pour into a medium pan and bring to a boil over high heat, stirring constantly. Reduce heat and simmer covered for 30 minutes. During this time, place ribs in a pot and cover with water. (The best are the baby back loin ribs.) Boil for 1 hour then drain and coat heavily with the BBQ sauce. Let stand for 15 minutes. Place under the broiler and brown on both sides. Transfer the ribs to a platter and serve. This BBQ sauce is also great on chicken and pork chops.

Peanut Butter Pie

1 8-ounce package cream cheese
1 cup powdered sugar
1 cup milk
1 cup peanut butter
1 cup whipped cream
1 graham cracker crust

In a medium bowl, combine the cream cheese and powdered sugar and mix until creamy with the paddle attachment of a mixer. Add the milk slowly, then the peanut butter and mix until smooth. To lighten the mixture, blend in the whipped cream. The consistency should be like a thick pudding. Pour the mixture into the crust making sure that the contents are even. Freeze the pie for 1 hour before serving which will set the peanut butter mixture. Place a dollop of whipped cream on each slice before serving.

SOUTH EAST
REGION

Grouse Nest Restaurant	South Bloomingville, OH
Gun Room Restaurant	Marietta, OH
Millstone BBQ	Logan, OH
Oak Room	Athens, OH
The Olde Dutch Restaurant	Logan, OH
Restaurant Salaam	Athens, OH
Ridge Inn	Laurelville, OH
The Sandstone	Logan, OH
Zoe's	Athens, OH

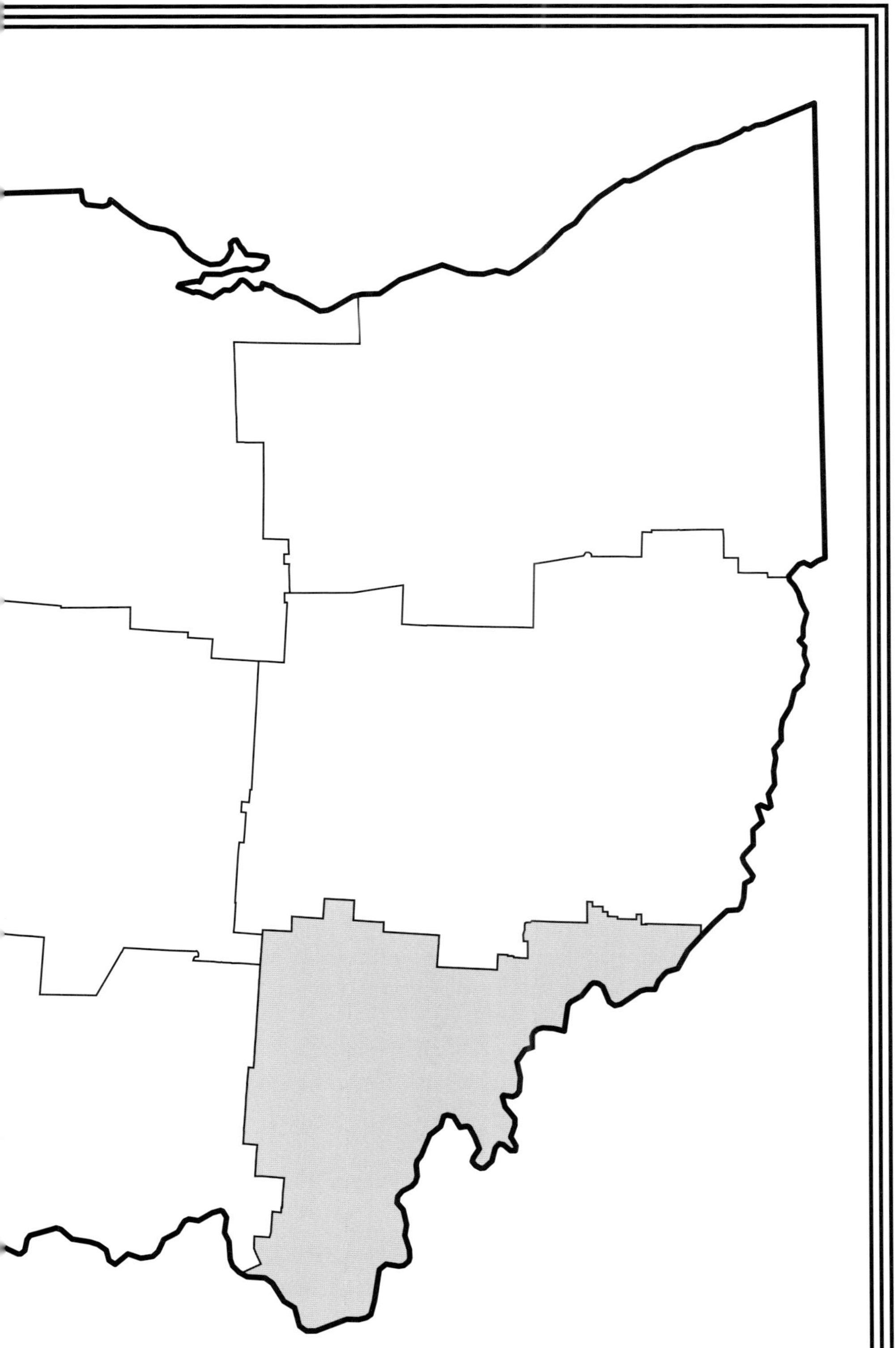

Grouse Nest Restaurant

South Bloomingville, OH

Hocking Hills Resort
25780 Liberty Hill Road
South Bloomingville, OH 43152
(740) 332-4501 • (800) 222-4655
www.grousenest.com

As one of the first restaurants in the area to offer fine dining in a casual setting, the Grouse Nest has long been a Hocking Hills favorite known for its unique culinary vision. Its American cuisine features wild game native to Ohio, like venison, rabbit, rattlesnake, quail, boar and catfish. And Chef Stacy Miller has a distinguished reputation for creating signature dishes with a gourmet twist. Only the freshest locally grown ingredients and produce are used, often being picked or caught the same day. This is something that owner Randy Strickland is proud of considering that commercial food suppliers are not conveniently located in the Hocking Hills area.

Since my last visit, the menu has changed, but they still offer the wild dishes (Venison Chili and Blackened Catfish, Jumbalaya Rattlesnake, and Lobster Ravioli), as well as Asian dishes. The talented Chef Miller is the creative genius who develops these exotic dishes.

An excellent meal must be followed up with the finest of desserts, and there are plenty to choose from including all of my favorites: Crème Brule, Chocolate Mousse and Smore's Cupcake. How perfect and simply delicious!

Below are a few of their most popular recipes that have been a part of the restaurant's repertoire for quite some time, and they have generously shared these tantalizing dishes.

Blackened Catfish with Pineapple-Papaya Salsa

Blackened Catfish Seasoning

1 tablespoon paprika
2 teaspoons salt
1 teaspoon onion powder
1 teaspoon garlic powder
1 teaspoon cayenne pepper
½ teaspoon white pepper
½ teaspoon black pepper
½ teaspoon dried thyme

Combine all ingredients and mix well. Blacken both sides of catfish fillets with seasoning. Place remaining seasoning in a glass container and store in a dry cool place. Makes about 3 tablespoons.

Pineapple-Papaya Salsa
3 tomatoes, cored and diced
1 fresh pineapple, peeled and diced
1 fresh papaya, peeled, remove seeds and diced
1 bunch green onions, sliced
1 bunch cilantro, chopped
2 jalepeno peppers, remove seeds and minced
3 tablespoons lemon juice
1 teaspoon chopped garlic
2 teaspoons salt

Fold in the tomatoes, pineapple and papaya gently with the remaining ingredients in a stainless steel or glass bowl. Chill. Top the catfish fillets with a generous portion. Makes about 2 quarts.

Catfish filets
3 tablespoons cooking oil
Rice, saffron, prepared

In a large pan, fry the blackened fillets in hot oil. Top with pineapple-papaya salsa (see recipe) and serve with rice. Saffron rice is recommended for this dish.

Wild Mushroom Strudel

½ ounce chicken or vegetable Stock
1 ounce shallots
1 ounce garlic, minced
½ pound wild mushrooms - Shiitake, Oyster, or other
1¾ ounces dry wine
1 ounce Boursin or Cream Cheese, both soft spreadable cheeses
Salt and pepper
½ ounce butter, melted
Phyllo dough

Heat the stock in a large sauté pan with the shallots and garlic. Add mushrooms and sauté until tender and liquid is reduced, or cooked down. Deglaze pan with wine and reduce until almost dry. Add cheese and stir until melted. Adjust the salt and pepper to taste.

Spread mixture on a parchment lined sheet in a pan to cool. When cooled, brush 3 layers of phyllo dough with butter. Stack the 3 phyllo sheets and mound the mushroom mixture along the long edge of each sheet of the dough. Roll strudel tightly, completely enclosing the mushroom mixture. Brush the top with melted butter. Place strudels in a 350 degree oven (conventional) or 300 degree (convection) and bake until golden brown, about 15 minutes. Makes about 5 servings.

Spinach Salad with Raspberry Vinaigrette

Baby spinach, bagged or fresh
Micro greens,
Strawberries, fresh, sliced
Candied almonds
Bleu cheese

Line salad plates with baby spinach and micro greens. Add fresh, sliced strawberries, candied almonds and Bleu cheese (see below) and drizzle Raspberry Vinaigrette (see below).

Raspberry Vinaigrette

8 ounces red wine vinegar
8 ounces rice wine vinegar
1½ ounces lemon juice
1 tablespoon dried thyme
1 tablespoon salt
1 tablespoon pepper
1 tablespoon minced garlic
4 ounces honey
8 ounces raspberry preserves, without seeds
12 ounces olive oil
1 pint salad oil

Whisk together the vinegars, lemon juice, thyme, salt and pepper, and garlic. Whisk in honey and raspberry preserves, blending thoroughly. Gradually whisk in oils, emulsifying the dressing and pour over the Spinach Salad. Makes 2 quarts.

Candied Almonds

1 egg white
1 tablespoon water
1 pound almonds, sliced
½ cup sugar
1 teaspoon cinnamon
Salt

Preheat oven to 400 degrees. Mix egg white with water and gently toss with sliced almonds. In another bowl, mix sugar, cinnamon and a pinch of salt. Coat the almonds with the sugar mixture and bake for 10 minutes, stirring about five minutes into the cooking process. Top the Spinach Salad with a generous handful of almonds

Crème Brulee

1 quart heavy cream
1 vanilla bean, split
4 ounces sugar
10 egg yolks

Preheat oven to 325 degrees. In a pan, over medium heat, mix the cream and vanilla together. Whisk sugar into egg yolks in a large bowl. Remove the cream from the heat, let cool slightly and slowly stir into the egg yolks. Pour an equal amount into 8 ramekins and set in a deep pan. Add hot water into the pan to cover halfway up the side of the ramekins being careful not to pour water into the brulee mixture. Bake up to 45 minutes but check the consistency so that it is firm. Makes 8 servings.

Gun Room Restaurant

Marietta, OH

101 Front Street
Marietta, OH 45750
(740) 373-5522
www.lafayettehotel.com

The Gun Room has long been a Marietta tradition conveniently tucked away in the historic Lafayette Hotel which is located on the bank of the Ohio River. Upon entering the lobby of the hotel, I felt like I had stepped back into time, especially when I saw the tall wooden pay phone booths nestled side by side in the corner. It was an era that I had long ago forgotten with the development of cell phones and other high tech communication options that we now rely on.

Upon further inspection, I discovered that the lobby and the restaurant décor were furnished in beautiful authentic antiques which boasted the elegance of a bygone era. Old movies of the 1930s and 1940s came to mind starring Cary Grant and Claudette Colbert, Jimmy Stewart and Myrna Loy where they appeared in settings such as this.

The hotel is named after Marquis de Lafayette, a French hero of the American Revolution, who was declared the first tourist to visit Marietta in 1825 and is reputed to have stood on the spot where the Lafayette would eventually be built in 1918. However, the Bellvue Hotel, built in 1892 and destroyed by fire in 1916, was the predecessor of the Lafayette.

Having traveled through Europe and stayed in ancient hotels and inns along the way, this hotel compares in its charm and authenticity. The sophistication of the hotel is matched by the cuisine of The Gun Room which offers excellent fare from around the world. If you enjoy history, fine dining and rich atmosphere, you will certainly enjoy the Gun Room at the Lafayette.

Fire-Roasted Red Pepper and Artichoke Dip

2 yellow onions, chopped
1 tablespoon granulated garlic
1 10-pound can artichokes, chopped
1 can roasted red peppers

1 cup white wine
6 pounds cream cheese
1 quart heavy cream
½ quart Half and Half
10 garlic cloves, minced
¼ pound butter, unsalted
1 tablespoon dry basil
1 tablespoon dry oregano
1 tablespoon dry thyme
1 tablespoon onion powder
½ cup salt
½ cup pepper
3 cups Parmesan cheese

Sauté onions and garlic in the bottom of a large pot on medium heat until they start to soften. Add artichokes and peppers and simmer for 2 to 3 minutes. Add wine, reduce heat to low and simmer for 3 minutes. Add cream cheese, heavy cream, and Half and Half. Whisk until the cheese is melted and incorporated, scraping the bottom of the pan to prevent scorching. Stir in all seasonings and Parmesan cheese to help thicken the mixture. Adjust the amounts of ingredients to desired number of servings.

Waldorf Salad

12 to 14 red apples, diced
½ gallon orange juice
1 cup celery, diced
1 cup raisins
1 cup walnuts
1½ cups mayonnaise
1½ cups whipped cream

As the apples are being diced, soak them in orange juice to prevent discoloration. Drain off the orange juice and mix the celery, raisins, and walnuts together with the apples. In a separate bowl, mix the mayonnaise and whipping cream and fold into the fruit until thoroughly combined.

SOUTH EAST

Millstone BBQ

Logan, OH

12790 Grey Street
Logan, OH 43138
(740) 385-5341
www.millstonebbq.com

The Hocking Hills is a popular playground in the state and features caves, walking and horse trails, zip lines and other outdoor activities for the family. Of course, where there is fun there must be food and the Millstone provides a wide selection of both.

Located in Logan right off U.S. Rt. 33, this relative newcomer to the area is clearly visible from the highway. It looks like a large rustic log cabin and, once inside, it takes on a log cabin décor, and it accommodates the large crowds that frequently gather for special events.

The Millstone is known for its southern smoked barbeque. All their meats are dry rubbed and smoked on site for up to 17 hours over a shag bark hickory. This process locks in the moisture in the meat and provides a melt in your mouth tenderness. Pork is not the only meat that is used in this process, the chef also smokes turkey and chicken which are quite tasty in wraps and club sandwiches, or on the bone and sliced.

The folks at the Millstone are certainly true to their slogan: "Where southern hospitality is brought north."

Baked Beans

BBQ Sauce

¼ cup butter
1½ cups onions
1 cup bacon, chopped
1½ pounds beef brisket, diced
3 cups molasses
5 cups Cattleman's BBQ Sauce
1 gallon ketchup
2 pounds brown sugar
⅛ cup dry mustard
2 gallons navy beans, softened

In a large pan over medium heat, melt the butter and sauté onions until soft. Fry bacon until crisp. Mix in the brisket, molasses, BBQ sauce and ketchup. In a separate bowl, mix the brown sugar and mustard, and add to the BBQ mixture. Combine the beans until thoroughly blended with the sauce. Cook on medium heat until beans are soft but not mushy and the meat is tender. Serve immediately and store remainder in glass containers Makes 8 quarts. This is a perfect recipe for the crock pot.

Coleslaw

2 quarts mayonnaise
1 1/3 cups white vinegar
2 cups sugar
2 tablespoons celery seed
1 head of cabbage, chopped

Combine mayonnaise and white vinegar. Add sugar and celery seed and mix together with the cabbage until the slaw is creamy. Add more cabbage if it is too moist or add more mayonnaise if it is too dry.

SOUTH EAST

Oak Room

Athens, OH

14 Station Street
Athens, OH 45701
(740) 593-8386

Located just a few blocks from the main campus of Ohio University, the Oak Room is a typical campus eatery - part tavern, part restaurant, part party place. This is a hang out spot before tests to settle the nerves, after tests to celebrate, late on Friday to connect with friends or early on a Saturday to study for the next week. On Sunday, students take a break because they are closed. But the one thing that this place has is really good food.

The Mac 'n Cheese is creamy because it is the blending of four cheeses with the richness of the Alfredo sauce. The Homemade Potato Chips have just the right mix of crispiness and saltiness, perfect for dipping in Ranch or Bleu Cheese Dressing. Baked Brie covered in honey is a delicious appetizer served with crostini. And the thick and cheesy French Onion Soup hits the spot as does the Chicken Breast Salad. In addition, there are Angus burgers and a variety of pasta dishes that fill the void in a college student's stomach without creating a void in his or her wallet.

Three Cheese Penne Mac 'n Cheese

1 pound penne pasta
Salt water
2 cups Alfredo sauce
½ cup Parmesan cheese
½ cup Monterey Jack cheese, shredded
½ cup Cheddar cheese, shredded

Cook the pasta in salt water until tender. Drain and set aside. In a saucepan or heavy skillet over medium heat, combine Alfredo sauce, Parmesan, Monterey Jack and Cheddar cheese. Stir until melted and blended well. Be careful not to scorch the mixture. Pour the cheese sauce over the pasta in a large bowl and toss gently until pasta is coated with the sauce.

Chicken Supreme

½ cup flour
2 5-ounce chicken breasts
2 teaspoons butter
6 sliced mushrooms, fresh or canned
1 tablespoon garlic, chopped
2 tablespoons white cooking wine
1 cup heavy cream
Salt and pepper

Place the flour in a bowl or plastic storage bag and coat the chicken so that it is lightly covered. In a skillet, melt the butter over medium heat and brown the meat on both sides. Remove from the pan and set aside. Sauté the mushrooms and garlic until tender and add the wine and heavy cream. Stir to thicken the sauce. Salt and pepper to taste. Serve the chicken on a bed of rice or pasta and cover with sauce. Garnish with a sprig of parsley.

The Olde Dutch Restaurant and Banquet Haus

Logan, OH

12791 St. Rt. 664 South
Logan, OH 43138
(740) 385-1000
www.oldedutch.com

The Olde Dutch Restaurant serves Amish inspired meals prepared with fresh ingredients and freshly baked rolls, bread and desserts. Not only can you order from the menu but a daily buffet provides a wide selection of fresh entrees, salads and soups. Manager Mike Erb is always willing to help guests find whatever suits their tastes especially specials designed to cater to children and senior citizens.

After enjoying a good meal, visit the roomy gift shop in the lobby that features many Ohio related gifts as well as beautiful handcrafted items. There is a sizeable section of reasonably priced toys to keep the kids occupied for the drive too. And be sure to visit the pet sanctuary next door to the restaurant where darling albino deer and pigmy goats are free to roam in a fenced area. Corn treats are provided at the site for a quarter from dispensers, so you are not only encouraged to pet them, but you can feed them too. If you have the time, tee off at the miniature golf course right next door within walking distance of the restaurant.

Rempel's Grove shopping complex, where Olde Dutch is located, features many shops, like the Logan Craft and Antique Mall and the Country Cupboard bulk food store, where you can browse at your leisure.

Sweet Stewed Tomatoes

1 10-pound (1 gallon) can of sliced tomatoes
2 cups of sugar

Combine ingredients and cook over medium heat for 20 to 30 minutes. Remove from the stove and let cool slightly. Serve warm separately or combined with other dishes, but you may have to adjust the quantity of the ingredients to suit the number of servings.

Women's Restroom

Olde Dutch
RESTAURANT
GIFT SHOP

Restaurant Salaam

Athens, OH

21 West Washington Street
Athens, OH 45701
(740) 594-3800
http://www.restaurantsalaam.com

This restaurant is not just a place to catch a bite to eat but it is a unique dining experience. The cuisine is inspired by the Middle East, North Africa, and India where the owners Hilarie and Mark Burhns travelled rather extensively. They are more knowledgeable about the pairing and use of herbs and spices in cooking than anyone I know, even more so than in many of the books I have read on the subject. When I met with them I received an in-depth education in the Mediterranean tradition of preparing food which was quite exciting since I love to cook and enjoy Mediterranean cuisine.

This quaint and lovely retreat is decorated in authentic Pakistani quilts, textiles, lamps, and mementos gathered during the owners' travels and life abroad. The decor adds to the warm and welcoming atmosphere of this lovely cove in downtown Athens, just a few blocks from Ohio University's main campus.

Before you visit, make sure you check out their beautiful web site which is choked full of information and great images.

Indian Spiced Cabbage and Cilantro Slaw

Hilarie shared the following recipe with the comment that, "At Salaam we love this slaw with our Besan (chickpea flour) Battered Fried Fish and Sweet Potato Fries. We use cabbage from our local produce auction or our wonderful farmer's market. You can whip this recipe up in no time and reap all the benefits of the abundant fiber and antioxidants that cabbage has to offer."

1 small head green cabbage, sliced as thinly as possible
1 small bunch cilantro, stems removed, coarsely chopped
¼ cup cumin seed (not ground cumin)
¼ cup black or brown mustard seed

In a large bowl combine the cabbage and cilantro. Place in a small skillet and dry-toast cumin and mustard seeds until they make a popping sound. Set the seeds aside to cool in order to make the dressing.

The Dressing

½ cup fresh lime juice
¾ cup canola oil or other vegetable oil
⅓ cup sugar
½ teaspoon ground cumin
½ teaspoon salt

In a small bowl, jar or food processor, combine lime juice, canola oil or other vegetable oil, sugar, cumin, and salt. Whisk, shake or process well. Add the seeds to the cabbage and toss with the dressing. At Salaam, we dress the salad to order, but you can dress all or part of the cabbage, as you like.

Vegan Harira

"Harira is a traditional soup from Morocco and Algeria, where meat, eggs and noodles are often added. Our fragrant vegan version, however, is a popular, healthy and inexpensive Salaam mainstay." (Hilarie Burhns)

1¼ cups of brown or green lentils
8 cups of water
3 onions, diced
Oil
3 cloves of garlic, minced
1 teaspoon ground ginger
3 teaspoons turmeric
1½ teaspoons cinnamon
1 teaspoon black pepper
½ teaspoon salt
6 cups fresh or canned diced tomatoes
6 cups V-8 juice
½ bunch chopped cilantro
½ bunch chopped parsley

In a saucepan, cook the lentils in water until soft. Meanwhile, brown onion in olive or vegetable oil until quite brown and soft. Add garlic cloves, ginger, turmeric, cinnamon, black pepper, and salt. Stir the spices around with the onions and garlic for a few minutes, then add tomatoes, V-8 juice and the lentils and the water they were cooked in, plus the cilantro and parsley.

Let these ingredients simmer for 10 minutes or so, stirring occasionally. Garnish with additional parsley and serve.

Ridge Inn

Laurelville, OH

16178 Pike Street
Laurelville, OH 43135
(740) 332-0300
www.theridgeinnrestaurant.com

Located in a sleepy village, Ridge Inn is a diamond in the rough. Not that the restaurant is rough, but you wouldn't expect to find such a delightful place in such a small town. Owner Jo Eaves and her daughters have worked hard to make this a place that people drive great distances to visit. Their motto speaks for itself: *"Where fine dining meets home cooking."*

The food is excellent and the atmosphere is comfortable. I've had the opportunity to visit a number of times when I am passing through the town and each time, the food is consistently delicious and the service is very efficient.

Jo has an herb and vegetable garden right outside the door and clips and harvests what she needs to make her dishes fresh and nutritious. I don't think you can get much fresher than that! She also features regular specials and live music to add to the ambiance of this contemporary oak structure.

As a family venture, Jo's daughters work side by side cooking, serving and generally delivering goodwill to customers who come in from out of town to enjoy the atmosphere.

Pecan Pie

¾ cup brown sugar
1 cup light Karo syrup
3 eggs
2 teaspoons butter, melted
1 cup pecan pieces
Premade pie crust

Preheat oven to 350 degrees. Combine the brown sugar, Karo syrup, eggs and butter. Blend until smooth. Gently fold in the pecan pieces and mix together. Pour into prepared pie crust and evenly distribute the mixture. Bake for 35 to 40 minutes until the contents are firm. Let cool and serve.

Chicken Wild Rice Soup

Whole chicken
Water
2 stalks celery, chopped
1 whole onion. diced
1 whole carrot, chopped
1 can Campbell's Cream of Mushroom soup
1½ cups milk
4 cups wild rice, cooked
Salt and pepper

Cover chicken in a pot with water and boil until tender. Remove from the pot, place in a bowl and let cool. Sauté celery, onion and carrot until soft. Set aside. Strip the meat off of the chicken carcass and chop into chunks. Combine with vegetables and add the soup, milk and rice. Salt and pepper to taste.

The Sandstone

Logan, OH

As of this writing, The Sandstone is no longer in business, which is unfortunate since they offered a complete menu with daily specials served in their elegant dining room. They also provided more casual fare on their seasonal patio which was a buzz with activity in this small town.

When I initially visited, Caitlyn Zahard, their head chef, was still a student at the highly regarded culinary program at Hocking College, and created excellent dishes from scratch. At that time, she provided me with the following delicious recipes, and despite the situation at Sandstone, I'm sure she has a bright future in the food industry.

Sandstone French Onion Soup

5 Vidalia onions, thinly sliced
5 tablespoons olive oil
2 gallons beef stock
4 cups Port or other good quality red wine
½ cup dry Sherry
2 tablespoons kosher salt
2 tablespoons cracked black pepper
Bread or croutons
Provolone cheese, thinly sliced

Sauté onions in olive oil on medium heat for 20 to 30 minutes or until caramelized. In a large pot combine beef stock, Port and Sherry wines, salt and pepper. Bring to a boil and add onions. Simmer on low heat for 1 hour. Serve with thick French bread or croutons and a thin slice of Provolone cheese that should melt into the bread.

Sandstone Alfredo Sauce

2 quarts heavy cream
1 cup white wine
2 8-ounce packages cream cheese
5 garlic cloves
3 cups Parmesan cheese, shredded
Salt and pepper

In a large saucepan, simmer the heavy cream and wine over medium heat. Cut cream cheese into small cubes and add to the cream and wine mixture along with the mashed garlic and Parmesan. Whisk frequently until the cheese is melted and all the ingredients have blended together. Adjust the amount of cheese to reach desired thickness. Finish with salt and pepper to taste. Serve over your favorite pasta or rice.

SOUTH EAST

Zoe's

Athens, OH

24 ½ East State Street
Athens, OH 45701
(740) 592-4443
Check them out on Facebook

Conveniently located in downtown Athens, this is elegant dining at its finest. The upscale atmosphere seamlessly combines a casual attitude, where either jeans or evening dress is appropriate. This is a perfect spot for a romantic dinner or to celebrate a special occasion.

Owner Scott Bradley had a vision for this restaurant a few years ago and has focused primarily on American European cuisine, but the menu also caters to a variety of dietary choices including those who are vegetarians and gluten intolerant. Fresh locally grown produce is used in season and each dish is prepared with care by a knowledgeable and experienced chef, often professionally trained by chef Bradley himself.

Scott's goal is to "provide Athens with the opportunity for high quality fine dining with professional service," and in my opinion he has succeeded.

Potato Pancakes

5 pounds potatoes, unpeeled and boiled
4 tablespoons of pound butter
1 1/3 cups flour
1 1/3 cups Half and Half
8 eggs, beaten
1 cup onion, minced
1 cup Gruyere cheese, grated
1/8 teaspoon parsley
Salt and pepper

Peel boiled potatoes when cool and mash with butter until almost smooth. Combine flour gradually and blend in. Add Half and Half, eggs, onion, cheese and parsley. Mix well and then salt and pepper to taste. Shape into 3 ounce patties, dredge with flour and fry in a skillet over medium to high heat for 4 minutes on each side until golden brown. Be careful not to burn the patties. Serve with an assortment of sides like chopped green olives, roasted red pepper, applesauce, or sour cream.

Maple Dijon Dressing

1½ cups buttermilk
½ cup cider vinegar
1 tablespoon mustard
½ cup maple syrup
1½ teaspoons salt
1 teaspoon pepper
2½ cups canola oil

Combine all ingredients except for the oil in a food processor and blend thoroughly. Gradually add the canola oil and blend again until smooth. Store in a glass jar and refrigerate. This is a tasty complement to many dishes.

Buttermilk Dressing

1½ cups buttermilk
½ cup cider vinegar
1 teaspoon mustard
1½ teaspoons salt
1 teaspoon pepper
2½ cups canola oil
1 teaspoon tarragon
1 teaspoon parsley
1 teaspoon chervil
1 teaspoon chives

A variation of the Maple Dijon Dressing can be made by omitting the maple syrup in the above recipe and reducing the amount of mustard to 1 teaspoon. Add the fine herbs: tarragon, parsley, chervil, and chives. Blend together in a food processor and store in a glass jar in the refrigerator. This dressing enhances the taste of salads quite well.

SOUTH EAST

FAMILY AND FRIENDS

Gladys Killmeyer Gillespie

Anne Killmeyer

Ann Milligan

Florence Masters Patterson

Leigh Paschke

Tasia Paschke

FRIENDS

Jan Head

Vicki Nichols

Amanda Foster

Karen Raybould

Sheryl Robinson

Lee Anne Raybould

Karen Patterson

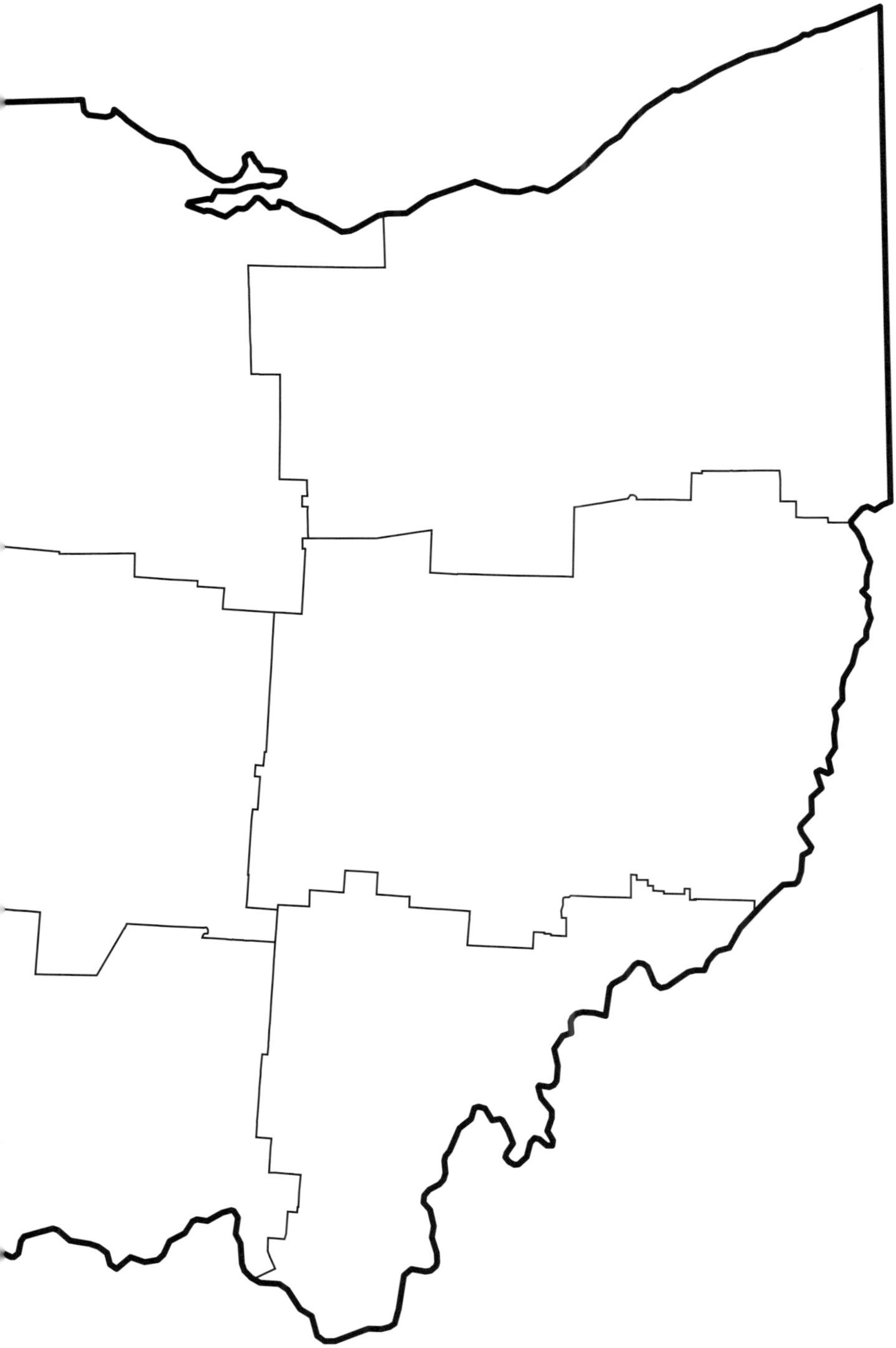

Gladys Killmeyer Gillespie

I am blessed to be a member of a family of great cooks. My mother, Gladys Killmeyer Gillespie, was a miracle worker in the kitchen. She pulled meals together seemingly out of thin air, though at times she used recipes she cut out of magazines or from one of her favorite cookbooks, especially her *Joy of Cooking* (Rombauer, 1931). She also drew from her own expertise and always created wholesome and nutritious meals. Even though my father, Fred, was a meat and potatoes kind of man, my mother was able to mix the menu up enough so that dinners were always tasty.

She often made vegetable soup from scratch, which was full of bite size chunks of firm veggies and a large meaty beef bone for seasoning. This was a perfect meal all year round. Her chunky potato pancakes served with sour cream and warm homemade applesauce were a real treat. Their aroma filled the air as she prepared thin silver dollar-sized cakes in hot oil. It was not until I had my own family that I appreciated how difficult it must have been for her to create an appetizing meal each day for a family of seven.

One of her many specialties was Beef Brisket that required a full day of cooking in order to be tender enough to cut with a fork. It was often served with creamy scalloped potatoes. Her Chuck Wagon Stew, one of my father's favorites, was a staple with its rich gravy. I don't know if she enjoyed cooking, but she certainly provided for our family.

Both of my grandmothers, Anne Killmeyer and Ann Milligan, also had their own specialties (Ann/e is a popular name in our family. My sister Stacie and I both share it as our middle names, and I consider it an honor to be named after my grandmothers.). The highlight of each holiday was Grandma K.'s tender turkey and moist giblet dressing. And Grandma M. contributed her delicious pies, along with her special Toll House cookies.

While I was growing up there wasn't much time for cooking lessons, so I picked up whatever practical tips I could from these special ladies.

During the research for this section of the book, I sorted through many of their recipes which brought back fond memories of good times. Over the years, I have used these recipes partly because they are time-tested and proven to be reliable and delicious, but partly because it is a way of remembering these strong and dedicated women that were so much a part of my life. In order to share their wisdom, I am featuring a few of their best here.

Beef Brisket

3 to 4 onions, finely chopped
4 tablespoons butter
4 to 5 pound brisket
Water
*** Bouquet garni with ½ teaspoon mixed pickling spices**

Cook onion in butter until soft and transparent, but not brown. Remove onions to a dish with a slotted spoon in order to let the juice drip back into the pan. Set aside. Place brisket in a Dutch oven and brown evenly on both sides in order to contain the meat's juices. Turn frequently to avoid burning. Make a bouquet garni and put aside. When brisket is thoroughly brown reduce heat, add ¼ cup water only if liquid is low. Note that too much will stew the meat. Place bouquet garni in with the meat and cover. Place on low heat on stove top and cook for 4 to 5 hours. Turn meat every 30 minutes and continue cooking until the meat is tender when pierced with a fork. Remove and place on a cutting board and let it rest for 15 to 30 minutes. Do not cut.

In order to make the au jus increase the heat to medium in Dutch oven. Add 1 onion and ½ to ¾ cup water. Salt to taste. Heat thoroughly.

Slice the meat diagonally, against the grain. Place on a serving platter and pour the au jus over the meat. Serve with scalloped potatoes.

* Bouquet garni – place 3 or 4 pinches or ½ teaspoon of mixed pickling spices (store bought brand name) and place in a small piece (4 x 4 inch) cheesecloth and tie up with a string. (Do not use a rubber band.)

Scalloped Potatoes

½ cup onions, finely chopped
2 tablespoons butter
1 can cream of celery or chicken soup
⅓ cup milk
3 cups potatoes, cooked and diced
¼ cup green pepper, chopped
½ teaspoon pimento, minced
¾ cup American cheese, shredded

Preheat oven to 350 degrees. Cook onion in butter until tender but not brown. Stir in soup and milk and heat thoroughly. In a 2 quart casserole dish combine potatoes, green pepper and pimento. Pour soup over potato mixture and top with cheese. Bake for 30 minutes. Serves 6.

Chuck Wagon Stew

1½ pounds stew meat, medium chunks
4 to 5 tablespoons oil
1 teaspoon chili powder
1 teaspoon white sugar
1 to 2 tablespoons flour
4 stalks celery, cut in 1 inch pieces
2 large green peppers, cut in 1 inch pieces
6 small or 3 medium onions, chopped
3 fresh tomatoes, cubed
1 small can V-8 juice
4 medium potatoes, cubed
3 large carrots, cut diagonally
1 small package frozen peas

In a Dutch oven, brown meat in oil turning frequently. Add chili powder, sugar, flour, celery, peppers, onions, and tomatoes. Stir and let simmer on low heat for 1 to 1½ hours. Add V-8 juice, potatoes, and carrots. When veggies are almost cooked add peas. A good stew needs meat to be well browned and vegetables to be cooked, but not mushy, with a sauce that is caramelized for best taste. Optional, add zucchini and mushrooms.

This was another one of my mother's specialties. Not only is it delicious, but it is healthy too. It was also a clever way of getting us to eat vegetables when my siblings and I were young.

Stuffed Green Peppers

4 strips of lean bacon, cooked and cut into ½-inch strips
1 medium-size onion, finely chopped
¾ pound lean ground beef
1 teaspoon salt
¼ teaspoon pepper
½ teaspoon sweet basil leaves
1 cup white rice, cooked
1 10.5-ounce can tomato soup
2 tablespoons parsley, finely chopped
4 large green peppers
8 tomatoes slices, cut ¼-inch thick
Freshly grated Parmesan cheese

Preheat oven to 350 degrees. Cook bacon in a pan until crisp. Drain on paper towel and reserve 2 tablespoons of the drippings. Set the bacon aside. Sauté onion in the drippings for about 5 minutes. Add meat and cook until no longer pink. Drain excess drippings and stir in salt, pepper, and basil. Add the rice and half the soup and cook slowly over medium heat for 10 minutes. Stir in reserved bacon and 2 tablespoons parsley and set aside.

Clean the peppers by cutting a circle around the stem large enough to remove the seeds and white membrane. Rinse and wipe the inside dry with a paper towel. Fill the shells with the meat mixture and place on a greased baking dish. Secure them so that they do not fall over during cooking. Pour the remaining soup over the peppers. Bake for 30 minutes. Remove from the oven and place a tomato slice on the top of each pepper. Sprinkle about 2 teaspoons Parmesan cheese over tomato slices. Return to oven and bake for 15 minutes longer. Makes 8 servings.

Gladys and Fred Killmeyer

Anne (Grandma) Killmeyer

My father's mother, Anne Killmeyer, made the best breaded City Chicken which was a real treat when I was growing up. Part of the novelty was eating it off of the skewer, but often it was so tender and crispy that it fell off the stick with the first bite. Years later, however, I discovered that it was not made with chicken at all, but with pork, which explains why this dish is sometimes referred to as "mock chicken."

City Chicken

1 pound pork, boneless cut into 1 inch cubes
10 wooden skewers, 4 to 5 inches long
2 eggs
1 tablespoon milk
1 cup bread crumbs, finely ground
1 cup oil
Pan cooking spray
Salt and pepper to taste

Preheat oven to 350 degrees. Push the meat on to each skewer until they are full. Beat eggs and milk into a medium size flat bowl, large enough to dip the skewers. Place the bread crumbs into a second bowl of the same size and shape and add salt and pepper. Dip each skewer in the egg dish and then in the bread crumbs until they are well coated. Let sit for 3 minutes and then repeat the dipping process. Pour the oil into a non-stick pan and brown the skewered meat over medium heat until brown on all sides. While they are browning, spray a 9 x 13 inch pan with cooking oil and place each skewer in a single layer. Bake in the oven for about 20 minutes until the pork is cooked throughout and no longer pink inside. Serve immediately.

Beef Tip Stew

- 1 pound beef tips
- 3 tablespoons butter
- 1 can of tomatoes
- 2 medium carrots
- 1 medium onion
- 1 green pepper
- ½ cup celery, diced
- 2 tablespoons salt
- 1 teaspoon chili powder
- ⅛ teaspoon black pepper
- 2 beef bouillon cubes
- 2½ cups hot water
- 2 cups diced potatoes
- Flour

Brown the meat on all sides in butter in a heavy 3 quart skillet. Add all of the ingredients except the potatoes. Cover the skillet and simmer for 1½ hours, or use a pressure cooker to cut down on cooking time. Add the potatoes and cook for a ½ hour longer. Remove the meat from the vegetables and serve on a platter. Place the vegetables in a serving bowl. Thicken the juice with flour and serve in a gravy boat.

Anne Killmeyer and sons.

Ann (Grandma) Milligan

My mother's step-mother, Ann Milligan, was an exquisite baker and always made our Thanksgiving pumpkin and apple pies. Her crusts were delicate and flakey, and she topped off her apple pies with a scrumptious cinnamon and brown sugar crumb crust. Her Czechoslovakian heritage certainly was evident when she made homemade pierogies filled with cheese, onions or mashed potatoes that would melt-in-your-mouth. And we were the grateful recipients of this culinary heritage.

Pumpkin Pie

4 cups pumpkin
¾ cup white sugar
¾ cup brown sugar
4 eggs, beaten
1 teaspoon cinnamon
½ teaspoon cloves, ground
1 teaspoon nutmeg
12 ounces (1½ cup) evaporated milk or 2 cups whole milk
4 tablespoons butter, melted
1 teaspoon ginger
1 teaspoon real vanilla
4 tablespoons flour
1 teaspoon salt
Dash of lemon juice

Preheat oven to 425 degrees. Mix together the pumpkin and both sugars and set aside. Mix remaining ingredients together in a blender and add pumpkin mixture. Blend well. Place in an unbaked pie shell (homemade or commercial shell). Bake for 10 minutes then turn temperature to 350 degrees and bake until done, about 40 minutes. Test by inserting a knife in the center. If it comes out clean then the pie is thoroughly baked.

Apple Pie With Crunch Topping

Crust
2 cups flour
16 tablespoons shortening (Crisco)
1 teaspoon salt
3 handfuls water

Cut the shortening into the flour until small kernel-sized balls are formed. Add the salt and gradually the water. Mix well and form a larger ball that is not gooey but easy to work with. Handle the dough sparingly or else the crust will not be flakey. Divide into two for two pies and roll out and gently place into pie pans. Cut off extra dough around the edge of the pan. Wrap up and freeze any remaining dough to be used later. Makes 2 pies.

Filling
5 pounds apples
¾ cup white sugar
¼ cup brown sugar
½ teaspoon cinnamon

Preheat oven to 425 degrees. Peel, core and slice apples. If using tart apples, add 1 cup white sugar. If not tart, use ¾ cup white sugar. And add brown sugar. Add and mix the cinnamon. Place mixture in unbaked pie shells.

Crunch Topping
½ cup butter, softened
¾ cup brown sugar
¾ cup oatmeal
½ cup flour

Cream the butter until smooth. Mix with the rest of the ingredients until it is crumbly. Sprinkle over the top of the apple pie mixture so that it is covered. Bake pies for 10 minutes at 425 degrees then at 400 degrees for 35 minutes.

Pierogies

3 to 4 cups flour
1 tablespoon salt
2 eggs
3 handfuls water
3 green onions, chopped

Mix all ingredients until a lightly sticky ball is formed and does not fall apart. Knead the dough until it is smooth and elastic. Cover with foil or wax paper so it does not dry out and let sit until the filling is prepared.

Filling

There is a variety of filling mixtures that can be used including cheesy potatoes or sauerkraut.

Cheesy Potato
8 potatoes
12 ounces sharp yellow cheese

Peel potatoes, cut into chunks and cook until soft. Slice cheese into hot potatoes and mash together. Place on a plate and let the mixture cool.

Sauerkraut
1 to 2 jars of sauerkraut
1 tablespoon oil

Wash sauerkraut. Squeeze and let drain in a colander. Finely chop and sauté in oil until it is dry. Remove from the heat and place in a dish to let cool.

After the filling is prepared take a handful of the dough and roll it out until very thin. Cut into squares and place the filling on each square. Firmly pinch closed into triangles and repeat with the rest of the dough using a handful at a time to avoid drying it out.

In order to cook, drop the triangles into salted boiling water and bring back to a boil (about 2 minutes) or until pierogies bounce up and down 2 or 3 times. No longer or they will be overcooked and will break up in the water. Remove with a slotted spoon or pour into a colander. Rinse with cold water and drain. Sauté in butter until almost golden brown and add green onions.

Chicken Paprikash

2 tablespoons butter
¼ cup onion, chopped
½ cup tomato sauce
1 teaspoon salt
1½ tablespoons paprika
¾ cup chicken broth
3 pound broiler or fryer chicken, cut up
2 tablespoons flour
¼ cup water
½ cup sour cream

Heat butter over medium heat in a large pan. Sauté onion until soft. Pour tomato sauce into the pan and add salt, paprika and chicken broth. Bring to a boil, stirring thoroughly. Place chicken pieces in the sauce and turn over to coat them. Lower heat and simmer covered for about 30 minutes until chicken is tender. Remove the chicken, cover and set aside. Mix flour and water in a jar and shake vigorously. Slowly pour into the pan and stir until the sauce is thickened. Stir in sour cream and add more broth if the sauce is too thick. Then place chicken back into the pan and simmer for about 5 minutes longer until thoroughly heated. Makes 3 to 4 servings.

Tom and Ann Milligan

Florence Masters Patterson

My mother-in-law, Florence, was a gentle and dear woman who received her teaching degree from Ohio State University and taught English and Home Economics in the Big Walnut School District for years. Her witty sense of humor would often change the course of a serious discussion into a laugh fest by simply remarking on something she had seen or telling a joke on herself. And her positive attitude helped her overcome many challenges she faced including the loss of two husbands.

One of the joys in her life was going out for lunch which we did often. The Timbers in Bainbridge or the Blind Monk Restaurant in Columbus were a couple of her favorites. She loved to eat, though it never showed on her tall slender frame. When John and I visited her home she would often make one of the following recipes for dinner.

Rice And Ground Chuck Casserole

1 green pepper, minced
2 medium onions, chopped
1 cup celery, finely chopped
3 tablespoons oil
1 pound ground chuck
1 20-ounce can diced tomatoes
½ cup rice, uncooked
1 teaspoon salt
Pepper to taste

Preheat oven to 350 degrees. Sauté the green pepper, onions, celery in oil until tender. Add ground chuck and cook until the meat is heated thoroughly. Stir and place all ingredients into a 2 quart casserole dish. Bake covered for 1 hour. Serves 6.

Sausage And Beans

1 pound of sausage
1 to 2 16-ounce cans of Navy or Baked Beans
1 tablespoon brown sugar
Pam cooking spray

Preheat oven to 400 degrees. Brown sausage in a no-stick pan. Stir in the beans. Add brown sugar and mix well. Spray a baking dish and pour in the meat mixture. Bake for 15 minutes until beans are tender and the meat is done.

Tuna-Noodle Casserole With Mushroom Sauce

1 teaspoon butter
1 tablespoon onion, chopped
1 10.5-ounce can cream of mushroom soup
1/3 cup milk
1 9.5-ounce can of tuna, drained
4 ounces of noodles, cooked
3/4 cup potato chips, crushed

Preheat oven to 350 degrees. Melt butter in saucepan. Add onion and cook until transparent. Stir in soup and milk, then fold in tuna and noodles. Place in a buttered 1½-quart casserole. dish. Sprinkle potato chips over the enire top. Bake for 25 to 30 minutes until thoroughly heated. Makes 4 to 6 servings.

Florence Patterson

FAMILY AND FRIENDS

Leigh Paschke

Both of my daughters-in-law, Leigh and Tasia Paschke, have exhibited impressive creativity and culinary skills in the kitchen and are keeping up with our family's cooking tradition. I am so pleased that as newlyweds, they are feeding our sons very well.

Leigh focuses on making nutritious meals to keep she and Josh healthy and fit. They subscribe to a rigorous lifestyle that includes daily workouts, regular hiking trips, running national marathons and even climbing Mt. Kilimanjaro in Tanzania. The following is just a sampling of what one finds on their dinner table. Whenever John and I visit we always look forward to tasting Leigh's latest creative dish.

Sweet Potatoes with Kale and White Beans

4 medium sweet potatoes
4 tablespoons olive oil
1 medium sweet onion, chopped
3 gloves of garlic, minced
1 fresh red pepper, chopped
5 ounces fresh kale
1 15-ounce can cannelloni white beans
Salt and pepper

Wrap sweet potatoes in foil and bake for 1:15 minutes at 400 degrees. Sauté onion and garlic in olive oil until tender. Add pepper and cook another 2 to 3 minutes. Add kale and cook until wilted, then stir in beans and heat thoroughly.

Split potatoes in half and serve kale and bean mixture on top of the potatoes. Season with salt and pepper to taste.

Condensed "Cream of Anything" Soup

1 cup cold milk
2 tablespoons cornstarch
1½ tablespoons butter
1 teaspoon chicken bouillon
½ teaspoon salt
Dash of pepper

In a small saucepan, whisk milk and cornstarch until well blended. Stir in butter, bouillon, salt, and pepper. Heat to a boil, stirring frequently. Simmer on low heat for one more minute to thicken.

Use this recipe as a foundation to replace one can of cream of anything soup. For instance, to replace one can of cream of mushroom soup, stir in a drained 4 ounce can of mushroom pieces to the base recipe as described above. To replace one can of cream of chicken soup, stir in ½ cup cooked chicken pieces to the base recipe. Or to replace one can of cream of celery soup, stir in ½ cup sautéed chopped celery to the recipe above.

Thai Coconut Curry Shrimp

1 teaspoon canola oil
½ cup onion, chopped
¼ teaspoon red curry paste (such as Thai Kitchen)
1 teaspoon sugar
12 ounces large shrimp, peeled and deveined
⅓ cup light coconut milk
2 teaspoons fish sauce
¼ cup green onions, chopped
1 tablespoon fresh basil, chopped

Heat oil in a large nonstick skillet over medium to high heat. Add onion and curry paste to pan, and sauté 1 minute, stirring occasionally. Stir in sugar and sauté 15 seconds. Add shrimp and sauté 3 minutes or until shrimp is done, stirring frequently. Stir in coconut milk and fish sauce; cook 30 seconds or until thoroughly heated. Remove from heat and stir in green onions and basil. Serve over rice.

Tasia Paschke

One night as I was preparing a traditional Mexican meal with chicken tortilla wraps, rice and refried beans, Tasia offered to make her guacamole dish. Recently married to our son Jesse, she wanted to contribute to the meal so she whipped up a tasty guacamole dish like a pro. One taste proved to me that it would be a hit on the menu of any Mexican restaurant. Here is the recipe and I challenge you to compare it to the commercially prepared brands. Not only does it taste authentically Mexican, it is easy to make.

Guacamole

4 avocados
½ teaspoon fresh lime juice
½ teaspoon fresh lemon juice
1 medium purple onion, finely diced
2 Roma tomatoes, diced
Salt

Peel the avocados and scoop or scrap the meat out of the shells and place in a bowl. Mash them with a potato masher or by hand with a fork but the consistency can be slightly lumpy. Roll the lemon and lime on a hard surface to loosen the pulp and create more juice. Cut in quarters and squeeze the juice into the mashed avocado meat and mix thoroughly. Fold in the onion and tomatoes until thoroughly blended with the avocado mixture. Salt to taste. Refrigerate for an hour and then serve with chips or as a side dish on its own.

Turkey Dip

1 pound package ground turkey
1 to 2 envelopes taco seasoning

1 10-ounce can of Ro*Tel diced tomatoes and green chilies
1 15-ounce jar of Tostitos Salsa Con Queso

Brown the turkey in a medium saucepan. Once thoroughly cooked add the taco seasoning, Ro*tel and the salsa con queso. Mix well and heat until the cheese is melted. Stir and serve with tortilla chips.

Tuscany Soup (Zuppa Toscana)

This is a popular Italian soup that Tasia makes from scratch adding her creative touch. She served it for Christmas Eve one year and it is absolutely delicious and very healthy too.

1 or 2 pounds ground Italian sausage (depends on how meaty you want your soup)
6 tablespoons Bacon Bits or cooked bacon, chopped
1 large yellow onion, diced
3 teaspoons garlic, minced
2 pounds golden potatoes or about 6 large white potatoes, sliced
½ bunch of kale
1 cup heavy whipping cream
7 cups water
3 cups chicken broth

Cook Italian sausage in a large pot. In the same pan, sauté bacon, onions and garlic over low-medium heat for approximately 15 to 20 minutes. Add chicken broth and water to the pot and bring to a boil. In the meantime, cut the potatoes in 1 inch chunks and set aside until the water and broth come to a boil. Add the potatoes and cook until soft, about 30 to 45 minutes. Slowly mix in the heavy cream. Stir in the kale and let the mixture cook for another 20 minutes until the kale cooks down. Serve in tureens.

Tasia Paschke

Jan Head

Jan is one of those friends that is always there when you need her. Quiet and reserved, she observes everything taking place around her then makes her own observations and shares her opinion. Not only is she a good friend, but she is a great hostess. Here are a few easy and hardy homemade dishes that will satisfy a few guests or a crowd.

Easy Pasta Salad

1 package of spiral or penne pasta
1 bottle Wishbone Robusto Italian salad dressing
1 small can sliced black olives
Garlic, chopped
Parmesan cheese, shredded

Cook the pasta according to the package instructions. Rinse and cool. Combine olives, garlic and cheese. Add the Wishbone dressing and mix thoroughly. Toss and serve.

Two Potato Au Gratin

3 large Russet potatoes, peeled and thinly sliced
Salt and pepper
2 tablespoons fresh rosemary
3 sweet potatoes or yams, peeled and thinly sliced
2 cups whipping cream
1½ cups Swiss cheese, grated
½ cup Parmesan cheese, grated

Preheat oven to 325 degrees. Arrange half the Russet potatoes in a 9 x 13 inch baking dish. Season with salt and pepper. Sprinkle

½ tablespoon of the rosemary over the potatoes and top with ½ of the sweet potatoes. Season again with salt and pepper and a ½ tablespoon of rosemary. Repeat the layering. Pour the whipping cream over the potatoes and cover tightly with foil. Bake for 1 hour until bubbly and tender. Sprinkle with cheese and cover with foil and let it set up for 10 minutes before serving.

Jan Head

Vicki Nichols

Vicki has been a God-send in assisting me in my publishing business. She is also the Stephen Ministry Director at a local church, so she stays pretty busy. In her spare time she enjoys cooking, oftentimes providing delightful meals for our working lunches. As the matron of a large family, she holds bake-offs with her grandchildren that not only add a spirit of competition in the kitchen, but also teaches them how to bake yummy treats. Cooking different foods and experimenting with various recipes is one of her favorite pastimes, often resulting in appetizing combinations that her husband Stan enjoys.

Homemade Lasagna

1 pound lean ground beef or Italian sausage
1 32-ounce chunky Ragu spaghetti sauce, Garden Vegetable or Mushroom
2 pounds cottage cheese, small curd
3 cups Mozzarella cheese, shredded (reserve 1 cup)
2 eggs, beaten
¼ cup Parmesan cheese, grated (reserve 2 tablespoons)
1 tablespoon parsley, chopped
½ to ¾ of 16 ounce box of lasagna noodles (about 10), cooked and drained

Preheat the oven to 350 degrees. In a large skillet, brown the beef or sausage and drain well. Add spaghetti sauce and simmer for 5 minutes then set aside. In a large bowl, combine cottage cheese, eggs, parsley, 2 tablespoons of the Parmesan cheese, and 2 cups of the Mozzarella cheese. Mix well and set aside. In a 9 x 13 inch pan, evenly spread ¾ cup of the meat sauce on the bottom. Layer with 5 noodles. Top with 1¾ cup of cheese mixture. Repeat layers of the meat mixture, the noodles and the cheese mixture finishing with the meat sauce layer. Top with the remaining Mozzarella and Parmesan cheeses. Bake covered for 40 minutes and then uncover and bake 10 more minutes. Cool for 10 minutes before serving.

Pineapple Upsidedown Cake

¼ cup butter
½ cup brown sugar packed
1 16-ounce can pineapple, sliced and drained
Maraschino cherries
¼ cup flour
¾ cup white sugar
2 teaspoons baking powder
½ teaspoon salt
¼ cup Crisco shortening
½ cup milk
1 egg
1 teaspoon vanilla
Whip cream

Preheat oven to 350 degrees. Melt the butter in an 8 or 9 inch round metal cake pan in the oven. Remove pan and add the brown sugar to the butter. Smooth the mixture evenly in the bottom of the pan. Keep in mind that this is the top of the cake. Arrange the pineapple slices over the brown sugar mixture without overlapping and place a cherry in the middle of each ring. Set aside. In a large bowl, combine flour, white sugar, baking powder, and salt.
Cut the shortening into the dry mixture until crumbly. Add the milk and blend well at low speed with a mixture or by hand. Add the egg and vanilla and beat until smooth. The batter should be firm. Spoon the batter evenly over the fruit. Bake 40 to 50 minutes until the cake is brown and springs back in the center. Cool 5 minutes. Run a knife around the inside edge of the pan to loosen then invert the pan, tap on the top of the pan and let stand one minute before slowly removing the pan. Let cool thoroughly. Top with whip cream and serve.

Vicki Nichols

Amanda Foster

As Vicki Nichols' daughter, you might say that the apple doesn't fall too far from the tree because Amanda loves to cook and try new recipes too. As the proud mother of five beautiful children, Amanda is quite thrifty and shares her penny-wise tips with others by teaching them how to live a frugal lifestyle. This is a different path than she imagined when she graduated from Ohio University, but she is making a positive impact on so many in these financially tight times.

She shared this recipe because it is a wonderful way of combining the pleasant taste of rosemary with the tangy citrus flavors of lemon and orange to spice up roasted chicken. Enjoy!

Citrus Rosemary Chicken

2 3-4 pound whole chickens
Seasoning salt and pepper
1 lemon, sliced in quarters
1 orange, sliced in quarters
1 teaspoon garlic, minced
8 sprigs fresh rosemary
8 sprigs fresh thyme
½ cup butter
¼ cup white cooking wine

Preheat the oven to 425 degrees. Lightly season the chickens with salt and pepper. Stuff each chicken with half the lemon, half the orange, 1 teaspoon of garlic, and two sprigs each of rosemary and thyme. Tie the legs together with kitchen string. Set the chicken in a roasting pan and tuck the remaining sprigs of thyme and rosemary between the legs. The butter should be distributed equally under the skin of the breast on each chicken along with the wine.

Additional garlic may be added. Roast the chicken for about an hour until the thermometer reads an internal temperature of 165 degrees. Let the chicken cool for 10 minutes prior to carving.

Perfect Apple Pie

Crust
2 cups all purpose flour
1 teaspoon salt
2/3 cups butter flavored shortening
6 to 8 tablespoons cold water

Sift flour and salt together in a large bowl. Cut in shortening with a fork or pastry cutter until pieces are the size of small peas. Add cold water 1 tablespoon at a time until pieces start to stick together and a firm dough consistency is reached. Form dough into a ball. For 2 pie crusts, divide the ball into two equal parts and roll into balls. Sprinkle lightly with flour. Using a rolling pin, roll each ball from the center to the edges until the pastry is approximately 1/8 inch thick. Lay the bottom crust in a 9 inch pie pan and add filling. Makes 2 9 inch crusts.

Filling
6 to 8 cups apples, sliced
1 tablespoon lemon juice
1 cup sugar
2 tablespoons flour
1 teaspoon cinnamon
½ teaspoon nutmeg
Dash of salt
2 tablespoons butter

Preheat oven to 400 degrees. Slice 6 to 8 cups apples, toss with 1 tablespoon lemon juice for tartness. Combine sugar, flour, spices and dash of salt in separate bowl. Add this mixture to the apples and toss until apples are covered. Add filling to the prepared 9 inch pie crust. Dot the filling with butter, or the batter may be melted and drizzled over the filling. Add the top crust. Adjust to make sure it covers completely, then crimp the edges together, with a crimper or by hand, to seal. Cut 3 or 4 inch slits through the top so steam can escape during baking. Bake for 50 minutes or until done. Let pie cool for about an hour before serving.

Amanda Foster

Karen Raybould

Karen is one of my long time friends and has been a great help with both travel books. Her specialty is her Sour Cream Coffee Cake that she generously makes for new folks moving into her neighborhood or sick friends, and for family staying overnight. It is always a big hit!

Sour Cream Coffee Cake

1 cup butter
2 cups sugar
2 eggs
1 8-ounce carton sour cream
2 cups flour
Dash of salt
1 teaspoon real vanilla
Pam cooking spray

Filling:
6 tablespoons brown sugar
2 teaspoons cinnamon
1 cup walnuts or pecans, chopped

Preheat the oven to 350 degrees. Cream the butter and sugar until smooth, then beat in the eggs. Fold in sour cream, flour, salt and vanilla. In a separate bowl, mix brown sugar, cinnamon and nuts. Begin to layer the batter and the nut mixture by pouring half the batter in a tube pan sprayed with Pam. Add half of the nut mixture and then remaining batter and top with the remaining nut mixture. Swirl with a knife. Bake one hour until toothpick comes out clean.

FAMILY AND FRIENDS

Easy Lasagne

This is a dish that Karen shared with me when I had company unexpectedly coming for dinner. I was panicked but her recipe helped me in a pinch, and my guests loved it. It's not only delicious but it's easy because you can quickly put together the layers since you don't have to cook, drain and cool the noodles beforehand.

1 32-ounce jar spaghetti sauce
1 24-ounce small curd cottage cheese
1½ pounds of Italian sausage, cooked
1 8-ounce package lasagna noodles, uncooked
2 to 3 3-cup packages of Mozzarella cheese
Parmesan cheese, fresh or canned

Preheat oven to 325 degrees. In a large bowl, combine the spaghetti sauce, cottage cheese and sausage. Mix well. Layer a third of this mixture and top with the uncooked lasagna noodles and Mozzarella cheese. Repeat with another layer and finish with a layer of Mozzarella cheese and topping with a sprinkle of Parmesan cheese. Bake uncovered for 1 hour. This dish can be prepared the night before and refrigerated until it is time to bake.

Karen Raybould

Sheryl Robinson

Karen's daughter Sheryl and her family are like a part of our own family. Sheryl works as an assistant for a local optometrist, but spent much of her life on softball diamonds and in gyms, first playing ball with her parents, Karen and Norm, and then watching her lovely athletic daughters, Stacey and Hayley. Sheryl and husband Rob are always busy and haven't slowed down much even though their girls are in college. Time is always limited so the following recipes fit in well with their busy schedules.

Tortilla Dip

1 to 2 8-ounce packages cream cheese, softened
2 bunches green onions, finely chopped
1 16-ounce jar mild salsa
1 package (2 cups) Cheddar cheese, shredded (preferably Kraft Classic Melts)

Spread the soft cream cheese evenly in the bottom of a small microwaveable pan until smooth using a rubber spatula. Sprinkle the onions until the cheese is covered followed with a layer of salsa. Top with shredded cheese. Microwave until cheese is melted. Remove and serve with tortilla chips.

Crock Pot Macaroni and Cheese

½ cup butter
2 cups Half and Half
1 can Cheddar cheese soup, undiluted
16 ounces Cheddar cheese, shredded
16 ounces elbow macaroni noodles, cooked

In a crock pot, combine butter, Half and Half, soup, cheese and noodles. Stir until thoroughly mixed, cover and cook on low heat for 1½ hours.

Easy Potato Casserole

2 pound bag frozen hash browns, thawed
½ cup melted butter
1 can cream of mushroom soup
8 ounces sour cream
2 cups Cheddar cheese, shredded
1 teaspoon salt

Preheat 350 degrees. Combine all ingredients in order in a 9 x 13 inch pan and bake uncovered for 1 hour.

Sheryl Robinson

Lee Anne Raybould

Lee Anne and Rick are also dear friends of our family. As a graduate of Ohio University, she is a busy middle school teacher in Columbus who specializes in science. As the mother of two active young boys, Ryan and Derrick, she has very little time to spend in the kitchen, so casseroles and crock pot cooking work well for her family. The following Squash Casserole is a healthy, quick and easy dish that can be made ahead, refrigerated and popped in the oven when needed. The Parmesan Dip, which is one of Rick's favorites, can be served with bread and meats or as a meal in itself.

Squash Casserole

Squash is delicious at any time of the year and can be used in a variety of dishes. There are two types, summer and winter. The summer squash is usually thin skinned and not as hardy as the winter variety. Choose a tender fruit but use it soon after purchase because summer squash does not store for a long period of time. Winter squash, on the other hand, comes in many colors and shapes with hard shells, except for butternut squash. Generally, the winter variety is available from fall to early spring, and usually stores well. Check all squash for water spots which indicates decay.

2 cups squash, acorn or butternut
1 cup evaporated milk
6 tablespoons margarine
1 teaspoon salt
2 eggs, beaten
¾ cup onion, chopped
2 cups Ritz cracker crumbs
1 cup sharp Cheddar cheese, sharp

Slice squash in half and remove seeds. Place on a microwaveable dish and cook until the meat of the squash is tender and a knife can be easily inserted. Scrape the meat from the shell, which is discarded, and mash until smooth. Combine milk, margarine, and salt together with the squash and add the eggs, onions, crackers, and cheese. Mix thoroughly. Pour into a buttered 9 x 13 inch casserole dish and bake until lightly browned, approximately 20 to 30 minutes.

Parmesan Dip

1½ cups milk
2 8-ounce packages cream cheese, cubed
1½ cups Parmesan cheese, grated
½ teaspoon garlic salt
1 loaf French bread

In a large saucepan combine the milk and cream cheese over low heat until melted. Add Parmesan cheese and salt. Heat thoroughly, stirring constantly. Then transfer to a fondue or mini crock pot. Keep warm and serve with cubed French bread.

Lee Anne Raybould

Karen Patterson

I have worked hard to duplicate my mother's and grandmothers' efforts in the kitchen. I enjoy cooking and have committed many of their recipes to memory so that now I easily combine and mix ingredients that usually work well together. I attribute that ability to the influence of these superb ladies.

When my husband John found out that he was gluten intolerant a few years ago my approach to cooking changed significantly. I carefully read the package labels and am surprised that so many foods contain gluten or wheat-based ingredients. I not only have to look for wheat, but also other forms of gluten. Some gluten-based ingredients are not so obvious. We have eliminated most gravy, soups, salad dressings, sauces, cakes, pie crusts, cookies and other products that I used to cook or bake so frequently. It certainly has been a challenge. However, we have proven that it is possible to live a gluten-free life, and the health benefits have been worth it.

Over the past few years, as we have visited numerous restaurants, we have found a growing trend toward the accommodation of special dietary restrictions, and not just gluten sensitivity. There is consideration for those who have various allergies, like peanuts, and others who are vegans and vegetarians, to name only a few of these special dietary restrictions. Many restaurants have specialized menus or have symbolic designations that inform the diner of "safe" choices. Of course, specific concerns can always be discussed with your server or restaurant manager.

The following Deviled Egg recipe is gluten free, but the Chocolate Cheesecake is not because of the graham cracker crust. However, a gluten-free crust can be made with a commercially packaged rice, potato or garbanzo bean flour. Bob's Red Mill produces a wide variety of gluten free flours.

Creamy Deviled Eggs

1 dozen eggs
3 tablespoons real mayonnaise

2 teaspoons yellow mustard
Salt to taste
Paprika

Place eggs in cold water and bring to a boil for 10 minutes. Remove from the heat and allow to sit for another 5 minutes in the hot water. Drain and stop the cooking process with cold water and ice. When the eggs are cool, place in the refrigerator for a minimum of 30 minutes until they are chilled. Carefully peel the shells without damaging the white portion. Cut each egg in half lengthwise placing the yolks in a medium bowl and the whites either on a platter or a deviled egg serving plate. Add 1 tablespoon of the mayonnaise to the yolks and beat with a mixer, then add the remaining mayonnaise and mix until the yolks are a smooth consistency. Mix in the mustard until thoroughly blended. Salt to taste. If the yolk mixture is too firm add more mayonnaise. With a small spoon fill each egg white with the yolk mixture. Sprinkle with paprika for color. Garnish with sprigs of parsley.

Chocolate Cheesecake

5 8-ounce packages cream cheese, softened
5 14-ounce cans Eagle Brand condensed milk
1 2/3 cups lemon juice
5 teaspoons real vanilla extract
5 graham cracker crusts
Genuine Hershey's Chocolate Syrup
Chocolate kisses

Place 2 packages of cream cheese and one can of milk in a large mixing bowl. With a mixer on high, blend together but not to the point of being smooth. Add two more packages of cream cheese and add two cans of milk. Mix again. And finally add the remaining cream cheese and milk. This time blend the mixture until smooth. Add the lemon juice and vanilla. Mix thoroughly until there is no visible liquid. Pour the mixture into each crust up to about ¼ inch from the top. Pour a thin stream of chocolate in circles on the surface of the cake beginning in the middle and working outward. Take a butter knife and run it across the chocolate lines from the center outward. Be careful not to go so deep as to cut the crust. Drop another dollop of chocolate in the center and place a chocolate kiss on it. Refrigerate or cover with foil to freeze for no more than 3 months. Makes 5 cheesecakes.

Herbs and Spices

Add a Little Zest to Your Cooking with Herbs and Spices

Herbs and spices can add that special essence to a variety of dishes if you know how to use them. These seasonings can be eaten either raw or cooked; however, when using herbs and spices in hot dishes, always add at the end of the cooking cycle to get the most benefit. Be careful not to overcook them. The following information is taken from my book, *Herbs for All Seasons* (ACW, 1999).

VEGETABLE HERBS

The following roots and/or greens can be used in a variety of ways.

BORAGE – The young cucumber-flavored greens are delicious in salads and pickles. Candied flowers are used in edible decorations or in fruit cups. The boiled leaves taste very much like spinach. And the entire plant can be steeped for a refreshing tea.

CHERVIL – The leaves are very similar to parsley except they have a distinctive licorice flavor and are preferred in cooking. The blossoms and seeds, which have a milder taste, can be added to spinach soup, eggs, salads, French dressing, fish and butter sauce for chicken.

CHICORY – The root is most valuable and can be steamed, roasted or fried like a vegetable. It does have a slightly bitter taste which lends a rich flavor to a beverage that serves as an acceptable coffee substitute.

DANDELION – This is considered to be one of the most perfect plants despite it's annoying reputation in the springtime. All parts of the plant can be consumed. The yellow heads can be made into a delicious wine, or added to salads, and even floured and fried. The young leaves can be used as greens for salads much like lettuce. And the roots can be dried and ground to make an excellent coffee substitute.

KALE – This is a highly nutritious green that can be steamed much like spinach or added to soups, salads or sandwiches.

LOVAGE – The leaf stalk and stem are very similar to celery and can be used as a suitable substitute for celery.

PARSLEY – The leafy portions of the plant are commonly used as garnish or in salads, eggs, potatoes, soups, and stews. However, the whole plant can be used to color wine, as an additive in sage cheese and in oil to prevent pest contamination.

PURSLANE – The leafy growth is most tender before the flowers develop. It can be used either fresh or frozen in dips or salads. And the whole plant can be steamed like a green or is delicious as an ingredient in dishes that are stir fried.

SORREL – The leaves can be steamed as a vegetable, and the flowers can be used in a tea.

HERB and SPICE SEEDS

Seeds from many herb and spice plants often serve as tantalizing additions when combined with a variety of foods and even beverages. The following partial list offers suggestions, but experiment and use your imagination.

ANISE – Add to beets, cottage cheese, cookies, pastry, pudding, salads and soups.

CARAWAY – Add to apple pie and roasted apples, black bread, cabbage, cookies, cheese, duck goose, Hungarian goulash, pork, rolls and bread sticks and sauerkraut.

CARDAMON – Add to cakes, candy, coffee, cookies, fruit salads, pea soup and rolls.

CELERY – Add to beets, cabbage, catsup, French dressing, gravies, pickles, salads and soups.

CORIANDER – Add to confections, cordials, pastry, pickles and sausage.

CUMIN – Add to cheese, meats, pastry, salads, sauerkraut, soups and spicy dishes.

DILL – Add to beets, cabbage, cucumbers, fish, gravies, ham, pickles, sauces, soups, sour cream, turnips and vinegar.

FENNEL – Add to black bread, fish, mayonnaise, salad, sauces, sauerkraut, soups and tartar sauce.

LOVAGE – Add to fruit salads, game, meat pies and stews.

MACE – Add to cakes, cookies, cooked fruit, meat, pastry and poultry.

MUSTARD – Add to boiled fish, cabbage, pickles, pickled onions, meats, salads and sauerkraut.

SESAME – Sprinkle on breads, in butter for vegetables, add to cakes, casserole toppings, cookies, creamed onions, fish, French dressing, lamb, noodles, pastas, rolls, salads and stuffing.

About the Author

Karen A. Patterson is a native of Pittsburgh, but has lived in Ohio for more than four decades. She attended Marquette University, graduating with a Bachelor's degree in communication and eventually earned a Masters in Fine Arts degree in nonfiction writing from Spalding University. At this writing she is working on her Doctorate in Education.

She has been a technical writer and editor for many large companies including the National Safety Council, National Eye Research Foundation, U.S. League of Savings Institutions, and Blue Cross/Blue Shield. When she moved to Columbus, Ohio, she directed the Communications Department for PriceWaterhouse Coopers and eventually made her way to south central Ohio where she directed the Marketing and Public Relations Department for Adena Medical Center. She continued in the health care field for many years as a consultant and national speaker.

Patterson has authored or contributed to numerous books including the first book in this travel series entitled ***Recipes From Ohio's Must Must Places to Eat.*** She has also written ***Allies Forever: The Life and Times of an American Prisoner of War***, a memoir about her father who was shot down Christmas Day, 1944, and was held prisoner in Germany until the end of World War II.

As a certified master gardener and syndicated columnist for the Gannett and Thompson newspapers, she has written about the practical side of gardening focusing on raising and using herbs in home remedies and in cooking, which resulted in her book ***Herbs for All Seasons***.

On her life's journey, she has travelled through Israel, Europe, Africa, the Caribbean, Central America and the United States, and tasted some of the finest food in the world, which she has described in numerous articles.

Patterson's work has earned her highly acclaimed recognition and numerous of awards. She lives with her husband John in southern Ohio where she teaches composition and communications at Ohio University.

Restaurant Index

Recipe Index

Herbs and Spices

Main Dishes

Salads & Dressings

Sauces, Dips, Etc.

Soups & Sandwiches

Vegetables & Sides

Other Books by Karen A. Patterson

Eating Your Way Across Ohio, 101 Must Places to Eat

Herbs for All Seasons

Allies Forever: The Life and Times of an American Prisoner of War